THE POCKET ADVISOR

A Family Guide to Navigating College

THE POCKET ADVISOR

A Family Guide to Navigating College

SUE OHRABLO, ED.D.

THE POCKET ADVISOR
A FAMILY GUIDE TO NAVIGATING COLLEGE

iUniverse books may be ordered through booksellers or by contacting:

iUniverse
1663 Liberty Drive
Bloomington, IN 47403
www.iuniverse.com
1-800-Authors (1-800-288-4677)

Because of the dynamic nature of the Internet, any web addresses or links contained in this book may have changed since publication and may no longer be valid. The views expressed in this work are solely those of the author and do not necessarily reflect the views of the publisher, and the publisher hereby disclaims any responsibility for them.

Any people depicted in stock imagery provided by Getty Images are models, and such images are being used for illustrative purposes only.
Certain stock imagery © Getty Images.

ISBN: 978-1-5320-5489-1 (sc)
ISBN: 978-1-5320-5488-4 (e)

Library of Congress Control Number: 2018909860

Print information available on the last page.

iUniverse rev. date: 10/10/2018

CONTENTS

PREFACE

Going to college for the first time can be an intimidating experience. You may not know what questions to ask or where to go for help. You may find yourself overwhelmed by the new processes, rules, and requirements that you're expected to understand. If your parents or other family members went to college, they might be able to provide some direction to you, but you may find that, if they've been out of college for a while, the information might be fuzzy or incomplete. If you are a first-generation college student, both you and your parents will be navigating the college experience for the first time and may find it a confusing experience.

Too often, I hear students exclaim, "My advisor is useless! She doesn't help me and doesn't give me the information I need." This book is intended to help you become self-sufficient in navigating the academic and administrative requirements that you'll encounter throughout your college experience, as well as to help you learn how to partner with your academic advisor and ask the important questions that will lead to your success.

It is my hope that, within these pages, you find easy-to-use resources and practical strategies that will help you succeed in college. Through this book, I want to join you as you begin your higher education journey and provide you the tools you need to make it a positive one!

How to Use This Book

While I hope that you read this book from cover to cover, there is no expectation that you do so. I've organized the book with easy-to-access chapters and topics so that you can find what you need when you need it. It is helpful to have all of this information as you begin your academic journey, but you may find that you will not need some of it until sometime in the future. For instance, in a year or two, you may find that you have trouble communicating with a professor or are considering dropping out. During those times, refer to the information I've provided to successfully meet those challenges. You can go back and forth through the book as it makes sense for you.

Tips for Students

As you begin your college journey, it is important to get prepared. Reading this book is the first step in taking responsibility for your own studies and actions in college. Think of it as prepping for the SAT ® exam or getting ready for an athletic competition. This book outlines the things you need to know and do to be successful. It is designed to help you understand what lies ahead, know what's expected of you, and find your way to the people who can help you. I encourage you to mark this book up; complete the tools, checklists, and activities; and keep it handy throughout your college career.

Tips for Family

Helping your child or family member get a successful start in college can be difficult. Your student is entering a whole new world, and it is understandable that you may not be familiar with the language and expectations within the world of higher education. If you have attended college, you have developed a sense of what your student will experience but may have forgotten some of the procedural details. If you've never been to college, the experience will be new to you as well as your student. I encourage you to use this book to learn along with your student.

I've written this book to address your student directly. This is not to ignore you but rather to set the tone, right from the start, that it is your student's responsibility to know and understand what college is all about. This is an important transition period for you. You've cared for and protected your student up until now and, suddenly, he or she is considered an adult.

Once your student becomes eighteen years old, the institution will hold him or her responsible for his or her decisions and actions. They will only communicate with your student, not you. In fact, in most cases, you'll need to have your student sign a release of information to give the institution permission to speak with you. My one strong piece of advice is this: *Don't ask your student to sign a release.* Work with your student and communicate with the institution through your student. If you cut him or her out of the process, you take away the responsibility and skill development that are essential to his or her growth and maturity. I encourage you to use this book in partnership with your student to understand the world that your student is entering and to provide the resources and guidance that will help him or her succeed.

ACKNOWLEDGMENTS

I would like to acknowledge my colleagues in the field of higher education who have provided me insight and support throughout the writing of this book, including Mirtha Bailey, for her expertise in financial aid, and Dr. Arlene Giczkowski, for her knowledge of student disabilities services.

I also want to thank my husband, Bob, who is a constant source of support and encouragement, and my daughter, Liz, who has successfully navigated her own college experience and is now working as a CPA.

Finally, I want to thank all my students who have shared a little slice of their lives with me. I am honored to be part of your journey and am always eager to celebrate your accomplishments with you.

CHAPTER 1

LEARNING TO SPEAK THE LANGUAGE OF HIGHER EDUCATION

1-1 Understanding Academia

Colleges can be intimidating places with lots of buildings, departments, and offices to navigate. Once you get to where you're going, you'll be asked questions that you may not be able to answer. The earlier you learn to speak the language, the easier it will be to communicate your questions and get your needs met.

Let's start with the basics. You need to know where you are, where to go, with whom you'll be working, and what you'll be studying. Below you'll find some terms and definitions that will help you get oriented.

Academic Institutions

Public: A public institution is one that receives a significant portion of its funding from local, state, and federal governments. Community colleges and state universities and colleges are examples of public institutions. Generally, tuition is lower at public institutions due to the government contribution.

Private: Private colleges and universities rely heavily on endowments (contributions from alumni and other private sources) and tuition dollars to operate. They are overseen by boards of trustees and have more flexibility in self-government. Private institutions may have smaller class sizes, and tuition tends to be higher than at public institutions since they do not receive as much financial support from government sources. Private institutions are either for-profit or not-for-profit.

> *For-profit*: These types of institutions may offer specific skill or trade programs, such as drafting, computer science, or medical assisting. They also may offer traditional liberal arts degrees that are similar to those offered at not-for-profit institutions. For-profit institutions are corporations that are designed to make a profit for their stockholders or investors.

> *Not-for-profit*: The primary mission of not-for-profit institutions is to educate students. They apply any income from tuition, endowments, grants, and other assistance directly into the operation of the institution. No profit is gained by investors or board members.

University: One of the defining characteristics of a university, as opposed to a college, is its size and scope of offerings. A university is usually large and is broken down into subcategories of colleges and schools. Universities include research as an important part of their missions and commonly offer bachelor's, master's, and doctoral programs.

College (stand-alone institution): Usually smaller in size and scope than universities, colleges may offer fewer academic programs and degrees and may not offer master's or doctoral programs.

College/School (within university): Students who attend a university will also be part of a school or college within the university. This will depend on your program of study, or major. For instance, there may be a college of business, a college of nursing, and a school of engineering within the university. For our purposes, it is not too important to know the difference between a school and a college except in those cases where a college has multiple schools within it. An example would be as follows: University X has a college of business, which houses a school of management and a school of accounting. The reason this is important to know is that universities, colleges, and schools may have their own admissions criteria and processes, as well as their own policies and procedures.

Department: Colleges and schools house one or more departments, depending on the size of the institution. A department will be made up of one or several related academic programs. For example, your institution might have a psychology department, or the psychology offerings might be grouped in with a department called Social and Behavioral Sciences.

Academic Personnel

The faculty members who teach college classes are referred to as instructors or professors, rather than *teacher*. In general, you can use the term *professor* to address faculty members, regardless of their rank. If a professor has a doctoral degree (PhD, EdD, DBA, etc.), it is best to call him or her *Dr.*, not *Mr.*, *Mrs.*, or *Ms.* Unless a faculty member has specifically indicated that it's okay to do so, do not refer to him or her by first name.

Faculty work hard to obtain rank by investing years of teaching, research, and service, and they appreciate it when you show them the respect that they've earned. Here's a rundown of faculty rank:

> *Full professor*: Top level of faculty rank. Full professors are full-time faculty members who tend to serve in leadership roles. Depending on the institution and departmental expectations, they are often engaged in research and may teach fewer courses as a result.

> *Associate professor*: Full-time faculty member who has conducted significant teaching, research, and service. Associate professors tend to take on leadership roles and are experienced in their fields.

> *Assistant professor*: Full-time faculty member in the beginning phases of promotion and tenure (if applicable). Assistant professors are responsible for teaching, conducting research, and engaging in service.

> *Adjunct professor/instructor*: A part-time faculty member who is specifically hired to teach.

Teaching assistants: Students, generally enrolled in graduate programs, who may teach large sections of introductory courses in collaboration with full-time faculty members or may coteach with full-time faculty members. Called TAs, teaching assistants may also offer small study groups and be involved in grading assignments.

Academic Terminology

You will hear many new terms throughout your college career. By becoming familiar with them, you will find it easier to communicate who you are and what you need to the various personnel within the institution.

Undergraduate: Students who are pursuing an associate's or bachelor's degree.

Associate's degree: Traditionally a two-year degree, often offered at community colleges. Associate of arts (AA) degrees are equivalent to the first half of a bachelor's degree and are designed to transfer to an institution that offers bachelor's degrees. Similarly, associate of science (AS) degrees are designed to prepare students for transfer into a bachelor of science program. Associate of Applied Science (AAS) degrees are designed to provide students the technical and professional knowledge needed to enter related careers upon completion.

Bachelor's degree: Also called a four-year degree, a bachelor's degree is made up of approximately half general coursework (general education) and half specialized, major-specific coursework. The two main types of bachelor's degrees are bachelor of arts (BA) and bachelor of science (BS) degrees.

Undergraduate major: A program of study that focuses on a specific topic or content area. Students are required to declare a major at some point in their undergraduate program, but it is common for students to change their major at least once. Some students choose to focus on more than one content area and opt to pursue a dual major.

Undergraduate minor: A program of study in addition to a major. A student who wants to focus on an additional area may choose to add a minor to his or her degree. A minor is not required; rather, it is a prescribed set of courses that usually takes the place of elective courses.

Graduate: Students enrolled in graduate programs have, in general, earned a bachelor's degree. There are a few exceptions, such as some pharmacy programs that admit students based on courses completed and credits earned.

> *Master's degree*: A specialized degree in a specific discipline. Generally, a master's degree takes one to three years to complete.

> *Doctoral degree*: A highly specialized degree that is usually completed after a master's degree. Some graduate programs have a master's/doctoral degree track that combines the coursework for the two degrees.

Degree-Seeking or Non-Degree-Seeking: A degree-seeking student (also called matriculated) has applied for and been accepted to a program that will lead to a degree. Degree-seeking students are eligible to apply for financial aid. A non-degree-seeking student (also called nonmatriculated) is not planning to complete a degree and is taking specific, individual courses for a variety of reasons, including personal interest, professional development, or transfer. Students are not eligible to apply for financial aid if they are non-degree-seeking.

Accreditation: The formal acknowledgment that an institution's or program's curricula meet a specific set of academic standards. The two main types of institutional accreditations are regional and national.

> *Regional accreditation*: Most colleges and universities seek regional accreditation as it is more widely recognized and highly valued than national accreditation.

> *National accreditation*: Institutions that offer career programs (such as automotive technology, dental assisting, and medical

records technology) may be nationally accredited. National accreditation is often awarded to technical schools with a very specific curriculum. Students who attend nationally accredited schools should inquire as to whether their credits will transfer to other institutions should they wish to do so.

Professional accreditation: Within institutions, individual programs and degrees may have their own professional accreditations. For instance, a college of business must meet an additional set of standards to be awarded Association to Advance Collegiate Schools of Business (AACSB) accreditation.

Academic Calendar

Semester

Most of the institutions in the United States use a semester hour system. There are three semesters within an academic year, most commonly referred to as the fall (August–December), spring (January–May), and summer (May–August). The fall and spring semesters are each approximately sixteen weeks in length. Students generally attend both fall and spring semesters, and the summer semester is optional to make up classes, take a lighter load, or work ahead.

Quarter

Some institutions operate on a quarterly system, with four quarters in an academic year. Each quarter term is approximately ten weeks in length. Students typically attend fall, winter, and spring quarters and use the summer quarter to make up classes, take a lighter load, or work ahead. The credit system for quarter hour programs is different from semester systems, with 1 semester hour credit equal to 1.5 quarter hour credits.

Term

This is a tricky one. The word *term* is generally used as a generic word for either semester or quarter. For example, "There are three terms in an academic year." However, occasionally *term* refers to a subset of a semester or quarter. For instance, a semester may have two or more terms—Fall 1 (eight weeks) and Fall 2 (eight weeks).

Institutions that break down a semester into smaller sessions may also refer to those sessions as *part of term* (POT). In order to accommodate students who enroll after the start of the term, some institutions will offer staggered starts that begin after the official start of the fall term. These staggered terms may be shorter in duration than their full-term counterparts but require more time-intensive weekly meetings.

Make sure to find out what your institution calls a term and how many sessions or terms are offered each semester.

Sample Academic Calendar		
Fall semester (full semester)	**Term 1**	**Term 2**
August–December	August–October	October–December
or		
Fall term (full semester)	**Session 1**	**Session 2**
August–December	August–October	October–December

By learning and understanding the terminology that is used at your institution, you can better navigate the system and understand the framework within which you are working. Use the tools within this chapter to get a clear picture of where you are and where you are going.

Getting Oriented Checklist

Sample

My institution: **Engaging State University** is a ☐ college ☐ university

My college/school's name: **Barry C. Smith School of Arts & Sciences**

   Location of main office/dean: **Building 4 Room 200B**

My department's name: **Department of Literature and Culture**

   Location of main office/chairperson: **Building 4 Room 111D**

My major: **Literary Studies**

My minor: **Philosophy (not declared yet)**

Complete the following information and keep it with you for your reference:

My institution: _____ is a ☐ college ☐ university

My college/school's name: _____

   Location of main office/dean: _____

My department's name: _____

   Location of main office/chairperson: _____

My major: _____

My minor: _____

1-2 Understanding the Rules of the Game

By the time you finished high school, you had pretty much mastered the rules. You knew what was expected of you and what would happen if you broke the rules or didn't do what you were supposed to. You had most likely even figured out how far you could push the limits without any negative consequences. When you get to college, you have to start all over again. Everything that was familiar is gone. In higher education, we love to use lots of acronyms and internal terminology, and we love to quote policy to you whenever we can. Unfortunately, there's a lot to learn right from the start. Knowing where to find important policies and procedures and knowing when to access them will help you make informed decisions and avoid any unanticipated problems.

As you would expect, most, if not all, resources are now online. This makes it easy to search and retrieve what you need. However, there's significant variance in how information is presented to you and how you can retain it for future reference. There are also a lot of people who work at colleges who do not like to use online resources and will be more than happy to hand you paper forms and brochures. The challenge will be figuring out where to find the information you need and how to keep it organized.

Let's start with some of the most important tools you need.

College Catalog

When I first started out as an academic advisor, I made it a point to meet with each and every one of my new advisees. I had a stack of catalogs ready at all times and would ceremoniously hand each student a crisp, new catalog as though it were the Bible. I'd encourage students to read it from cover to cover and to keep it with them until after they'd received their diploma. And I meant it. The same goes for you, although we need to approach it in a different way. I don't know of any colleges that provide their students with a hard copy of the catalog anymore. If you are lucky enough to get one, take it. The philosophy's the same, though. Within those pages is critical information that you'll need to know—or at least know where to find.

How to Find the Catalog

The easiest way to find the catalog is to go to the institution's home page and type in "catalog"in the search bar. Depending on the size of the institution, you might see several choices in the results. Look for the undergraduate catalog, and make sure it is the right one for the right school or college and the right year.

Another good way to find the catalog is to search for or navigate to "Student Services" or "Student Resources." Look for the catalog that corresponds to the year that you began your college studies. Colleges will refer to either your catalog term or your catalog year. See below for an example of how your catalog term or year is determined.

First Semester in Program	Catalog Term	Catalog Year
Fall 2018	Fall 2018	2018–2019
Spring 2019	Spring 2019	2018–2019
Summer 2019	Summer 2019	2018–2019

How to Use the Catalog

The first thing to do is to review the table of contents. Make note of the information that you'll need as you go through your program. Pay close attention to the following important sections.

Admissions

In addition to being admitted to the institution, some programs will require a separate application to the college or school of your choice. Some of these applications are due at the same time as the institution's application, while others may be due months (or years) later. The more competitive the program is, the more likely that a secondary application will be required. It is possible to be admitted to the institution, begin taking classes toward your intended degree, and then be required to apply for admission to your desired program. This may happen as late as one to two years after you have started college. Review the catalog to determine whether there is more than one application process.

Academic Programs

In this section, you'll find all of your degree requirements, including descriptions of general education and major requirements. We'll get more into detail about that in the academic advising section of this book, which can be found in chapter 3. You'll also find course descriptions in this area, which are an important tool for planning your course schedule each semester.

Policies and Procedures

This is a critically important section of the catalog. When advising students, I tell them that, before they make any decisions, they should consult the policies and procedures section of the catalog. It's better to know "what would happen if …" rather than ask "what's going to happen now that …"

Keep in mind the following things to look for:

- grading policy
- attendance policy
- incompletes/withdrawals
- leaves of absence
- medical withdrawals
- payment policies
- graduation requirements

Important to Know

(*While the information below is standard practice, make sure to confirm your institution's policy on catalog year.*)

- Your catalog year or term begins with the first semester in which you enroll in classes, not when you're admitted.
- Catalogs run from the fall semester to the end of the summer of that year.
- Your curriculum (program requirements) is "locked in" by your catalog year or term. If you remain continuously enrolled, the requirements will not change (except for a rare substitution of a course or two, which will not negatively impact you).

Student Handbook

The student handbook can be found as part of the catalog or as a stand-alone document. By searching "student handbook," you should be able to locate it pretty quickly. Generally, the student handbook includes all the policies that govern your behavior as a student, including the following:

- alcohol use
- health documentation
- copyright
- computer use
- animals
- hazing
- plagiarism / academic dishonesty
- residential life
- smoking / tobacco use
- theft
- sexual misconduct
- judicial processes

Important to Know

Failure to read and understand the policies set forth in the catalog and student handbook does not exempt you from the policies. "I didn't know" or "Nobody told me" is not a viable defense.

Syllabus

In each class you take, you will be provided a syllabus. Read it carefully and often. The syllabus contains the professor's expectations and policies. These can vary from one professor to the next, so it is important to understand what each professor expects. Within the syllabus, you will find information about attendance, grading, class participation, communication, and office hours. These are some commonly asked questions:

- Who is my professor?
- What books will I need for this class?
- Where is my professor's office? What are his or her phone number and email address?
- When can I go see my professor?
- How many points do I need to earn an A? How will I know if I'm failing?
- What happens if I have to miss class?
- Will I have to work in a group in this class?
- What is the professor's policy on cheating?

Learn more about locating and understanding academic expectations in chapter 3.

Departmental Websites

You should bookmark the websites of important departments. Below, you'll find a list of departments and the types of information you may find on their websites. See chapter 3 for additional questions you may wish to research and explore.

Financial Aid

- How many credits do I need to be enrolled in to receive aid?
- What type of money is available to me? What are grants, loans, and scholarships?
- What happens if I fail one or more courses?
- What are the eligibility criteria for receiving financial aid?

Registrar

- How do I change my contact information?
- When is registration?
- How do I register for or drop a course?
- How do I get a copy of my transcript?
- When is commencement? How do I participate?

College/School

- What programs are offered?
- What unique policies does the college or school have?
- What resources are available to me?
- Whom do I contact for help?

Academic Department

- What majors and minors are offered?
- What are the degree requirements?
- What courses are in my major? (Note: This resource should be used only in your first semester, as curriculum guides are often used as a marketing tool. If the program changes requirements for future students, your curriculum will not change. We'll discuss this more in the academic advising section.)

Student Affairs

- What clubs and activities are offered at this institution?
- What services are available to support me?
- What do I do if I have a conflict with my roommate?

Develop a system that works best for you. Bookmark websites. Print pages and highlight pertinent information. Take notes. After reviewing these resources, use the following as a quick reference sheet. If you can't find the answer, ask an academic advisor for help.

Locating Policies and Procedures

Information/Question	Resource	Notes
Example: Financial Aid Satisfactory Academic Progress (SAP)	www.university.edu/finaid/SAP	Must pass 2/3 of attempted credits. Ws and Fs impact financial aid eligibility
Registrar's Office (student records and registration)		
Academic Calendar		
Drop/Withdrawal Policy		
Refund Policy		
Financial Aid		
School/College Site		
Department Site		
Student Handbook		
Plagiarism / Academic Dishonesty		
Leave of Absence/ Catalog Year		
Academic Standing (Program specific)		
Academic Standing / Progress (Institutional)		
Alcohol Use		
Computer Use		
Other		

1-3 Who's Who and What They Do

There are many great resources available to you as a college student, but you need to know what they are and where to find them. As you travel around campus trying to locate these resources, you may find many of their offices in the same building, but don't be surprised if they're scattered across campus. If you're searching online, the offices you're looking for should be easily accessible by searching the office name or using a key word. If you are attending college on campus, make sure to know where to find information online and in person.

Admissions

The admissions office is responsible for processing your application for admission to the institution. Depending on the size and complexity of your institution, there may also be an admissions department within a specific college or school. Make sure to find out where to locate information about your admissions status and whom you should contact with any questions you have. Use the "Admissions Checklist" to keep track of the items you need to be admitted into the institution and program you want.

Admissions Status

When you apply to an institution, you will be required to submit multiple documents to be reviewed. Some examples of those documents are as follows:

1. Application
2. Application fee
3. Transcripts from high school and previous colleges (final, official)
4. Test scores (e.g., SAT ® or ACT ®)
5. Essay
6. Recommendation(s)
7. Proof of residency (state-run institutions)

Your admissions materials will be compiled into an admissions file by personnel in the admissions office and provided to reviewers who will make a decision regarding your admission. The reviewers may be admissions managers, faculty, or department chairs. An admissions committee comprising representatives from several areas of the institution may also be involved. Upon review of your materials, one of several admissions statuses will be awarded to you. While there may be variation in the terms used, most institutions will have admissions statuses that indicate how far along you are in completing the admissions process.

- *Full admission*: The file is complete. No further information is needed. Financial aid can be awarded and disbursed upon enrollment.
- *Provisional admission*: There is enough information to admit you, but outstanding items need to be submitted, often referred to internally as "missing docs." A common example of a missing doc is the final, official transcript. If you apply to college while you're still in high school (or another college), the transcript you submit at first may not be official (issued from the school) or final (including all grades and indicating notation of graduation). Even though you may have already sent your transcript, you may need to send a second one once you graduate from high school. Financial aid cannot be disbursed until full admission is achieved. Students who don't meet conditions of provisional admission may be blocked from further registration until all items have been received. Make sure to find out what is missing and the deadline for submitting remaining documents.
- *Conditional admission*: You have been admitted but with specific conditions that must be met. Conditions may include a prescribed number of credits to take in the first semester, a minimum GPA to be achieved, additional testing or essay(s), or participation in a student support program. Failure to comply with the conditions set forth in the admissions offer may result in the retraction of your admission.

Competitiveness

Most institutions will list minimum requirements for admission, including high school GPA and test scores. However, simply meeting the minimum requirements does not guarantee you admission. Some institutions and programs are highly competitive and may have more qualified applicants than they do seats. Find out how competitive your institution or program is so that you can have realistic expectations regarding admission.

Secondary Application

Yes, you've been admitted—to the institution. But have you been admitted to the program you want? Institutions often have multiple admissions processes and criteria, depending on supply and demand or program competitiveness. Make sure to find out if the program you want requires a separate application. I have had the unpleasant task of telling juniors who were excited to start their major courses that they had not been admitted to the program; in fact, they'd never applied. Don't let this happen to you.

In general, highly competitive programs, such as health sciences (especially nursing), have a multiple-application or tiered-admission process. Also, universities with upper division (junior/senior) programs housed within colleges and schools may require a separate application. When you begin the admission process, make sure to ask, "Is there a separate application I need to complete to be admitted to the program that I want?"

Admissions Checklist

To be admitted to the institution, I need to meet the following eligibility requirements:

☐ High school GPA: _____

☐ Transfer GPA (if applicable): _____

☐ Minimum test scores: _____

☐ Foreign language: _____

☐ Other: _____

To be admitted to the institution, I need to submit the following:

☐ Application
☐ Application fee
☐ Transcripts from high school and/or previous colleges (final, official)
☐ Test scores (e.g., SAT® or ACT®) (official)
☐ Essay
☐ Recommendation(s)
☐ Proof of residency (state-run institutions)
☐ Other: _____

My current application status:

☐ Have not applied
☐ Applied but awaiting decision
☐ Provisionally admitted

If provisionally admitted, list missing items and plans for submission:

Missing Items	**Due Date and Notes**
☐ Application	
☐ Application fee	
☐ Transcripts from high school and/or previous colleges (final, official)	
☐ Test scores (e.g., SAT® or ACT®) (official)	
☐ Essay	
☐ Recommendation(s)	
☐ Proof of residency (state-run institutions)	
☐ Other:	

☐ Fully admitted
☐ Other: _____

To be admitted to the college, school, or program of my choice:

I □ do □ do not need a separate application.

If yes, by what date does the application have to be submitted?

_____

If yes, where can I locate the secondary application?

_____

To be admitted to the college, school, or program of my choice, I need to meet the following additional eligibility requirements:

□ High school GPA: _____

□ Transfer GPA (if applicable): _____

□ Minimum test scores: _____

□ Foreign language: _____

□ Other: _____

Registrar

The registrar is the office that controls all things having to do with your academic records. Your grades, transcripts, and registrations are all processed through the registrar's office. The registrar is also responsible for the conferral of degrees and coordination of commencement ceremonies. The registrar's office can help you with many functions.

- name or address change
- official transcripts
- posting of grades
- degree audits
- academic calendar (term start; end dates; drop, add, and withdrawal dates)
- registration dates
- enrollment verification and loan deferments
- forms (major change; drop, add, or withdrawal; data change)
- Family Educational Rights and Privacy Act (FERPA) guidelines
- student IDs
- Student Right-to-Know Act information about overall graduation rates and enrollment

- degree application and conferral
- graduation ceremony (commencement) information

Some larger institutions may not house all those functions in the registrar's office. If you're not sure where to go, the registrar should be able to point you in the right direction.

Financial Aid

The financial aid office is a critical resource for many students. This office reviews student eligibility for multiple types of aid, including grants, loans, and scholarships. Since the financial aid office must adhere to state and federal guidelines for awarding and disbursing aid, their policies, procedures, and deadlines may seem rigid and inflexible. Students are often frustrated by the bureaucracy that is involved when working with the financial aid office and are prone to complain about lack of service or information. Please be patient and avoid taking out your frustration on financial aid personnel. They are trying to help you but have to do so under a very specific set of guidelines. Due to the complex nature of applying for and receiving financial aid, I recommend compiling a list of questions to discuss with a financial aid counselor.

Some important terms and policies are discussed below:

> *Grants*: State or federal monies that are awarded based on your financial need. They are applied toward the overall cost of your tuition and fees to help reduce or eliminate out-of-pocket expenses.

> *Loans*: Money borrowed to cover the cost of tuition, fees, room and board, and living expenses. This money helps to fill the gap between the cost of attendance and any grants you may be awarded. Loan repayment begins after a set period of nonenrollment. For some loans (unsubsidized), you may be responsible for paying interest while still enrolled.

> *Emergency loans*: Some institutions offer emergency loans to students who are in immediate, dire need of money. These

short-term, small loans may be used for buying books, getting food, or paying rent. They are designed to get students through a short-term financial difficulty.

Scholarships: Free money based on financial need, academic achievement, athletic ability, or any number of qualifying criteria. There are two types of scholarships—private and institutional. Private scholarships are awarded from outside agencies and organizations. This money is paid directly to you, the student, or to the institution. Institutional scholarships are funded by the college or university. I strongly encourage you to explore all scholarship opportunities with your financial aid counselor and through a comprehensive Internet search. There are millions of dollars that go unawarded each year because students do not apply for available funds. Even if you don't think you qualify or have a chance, go ahead and apply. If no better qualified candidates apply, you may be awarded the scholarship anyway!

Student employment: Students may be awarded a certain dollar amount that can be earned through working at an institutionally coordinated on-campus or community job. Most commonly, this is referred to as College Work-Study, or CWS.

Satisfactory Academic Progress (SAP): This is a very important policy to understand. Your eligibility to receive financial aid will be evaluated each year based on your progress toward degree completion. If you attempt a course but do not complete it (due to drops, withdrawals, or failing grades), your eligibility for aid may be negatively impacted. SAP review criteria include credits attempted versus credits earned each year and throughout the life of your degree, as well as GPA, academic standing, and overall credits attempted. Make sure to discuss SAP with a financial aid counselor and understand what is expected of you.

Return of Title IV Funds: Students who borrow money from loans may be required to repay some or all of the borrowed money in the event that they drop or withdraw from some or all of their courses. If you have received loan money, make sure to consult a financial aid counselor before deciding to drop or withdraw from classes.

Bursar

The bursar's office is responsible for collecting payments for tuition, fees, and other expenses such as room and board. Any financial aid that you are awarded will be applied to your total costs. If there is a remaining out-of-pocket balance, you are responsible for paying it to the bursar's office. The way you can remember the difference between financial aid and the bursar is that money coming *to* you comes from financial aid, while money coming *from* you goes to the bursar. Following are some important things to know about the bursar's office.

Payment plans: Some institutions will provide payment plans for students to pay their bills. These plans may require regular payments on a monthly or quarterly basis.

Payment policy: Find out when your bill is due. Don't assume that because you are planning to receive financial aid that everything is taken care of. It is your responsibility to make sure that the bursar's office is aware of any aid that you are awarded and to pay the balance. Adhere to the due date and learn the consequences of late payment. A common practice, especially among state institutions, is to drop students from all their courses for nonpayment. It is a terrifying experience that may leave you scrambling to find courses during the first week of the semester. On the other hand, don't assume you will be dropped for nonpayment. If you decide not to attend and do not pay your bill, there is a chance that your registration will remain intact, and as a result, you will still be responsible for the bill and will receive F's in your courses. If you decide not to attend, make sure to formally drop your courses and withdraw from the institution.

Collections: Just as with any other debt, institutions have a process for collecting monies owed. Late payments may result in registration holds, which will prevent you from registering for future terms or possible registration reversal. Students who owe money will not be able to obtain any official documents from the institution, such as transcripts, enrollment verifications, or specialized letters. Thirty-, sixty-, and ninety-day notices may be sent to students to collect debt. The college may have an internal collections department, but if the debt is very delinquent, it may be referred to an external collection agency. If you owe a balance, please make sure to communicate with the bursar's office and make arrangements for payment. Ignoring the debt only makes it worse. The bursar's office wants to help you resolve your debt and successfully complete your studies.

One-Stop Shop

Many institutions have a centralized office that can help students with a variety of issues, including admissions, registration, financial aid, and payments. They are generically known as a one-stop shop but might have other names such as the answer center or help desk. These offices help students with common questions, forms, and processes. By utilizing them, you can avoid running around trying to locate each of these offices separately. If you are not sure if your institution has a one-stop shop, just ask!

Tutoring/Testing

While these are two separate functions, tutoring and testing are often located within the same department or close to each other. You may find them near the student support or student success center, as they are related to student success.

> *Tutoring*: Students may have access to free tutoring services in a variety of subject areas. Common areas include math and writing. Tutors may be peer undergraduate students, graduate students, or professional tutors, such as retired professors. If you find yourself in need of some additional academic support, seek out the tutoring center for help.

Testing: The testing office offers a variety of testing services to students, which may include the following:

- placement tests in the areas of reading, writing, and mathematics
- standardized tests such as the SAT ® or ACT ®
- professional testing such as graduate school admissions tests (GMAT ®, GRE ®, LSAT ®)
- College-Level Examination Program (CLEP ®) test, which allows students to earn credit for prior knowledge and experience
- foreign-language proficiency tests that allow a student to be exempt or earn credit for language proficiency
- class-specific tests for students who may have missed an in-class test or may require additional time as approved by the office for students with disabilities

Student Support Center

Institutions want you to succeed! As a result, they may provide you multiple services in one department in order to meet your academic needs. A student support or student success department is a great resource to get help with any academic challenges you may be having or to obtain resources that will help you succeed. These are some common services in a student support center:

- tutoring
- testing
- writing lab
- math lab
- computers
- freshman seminar or first year experience support

Academic Advising

Academic advising is an important way to successfully navigate your college career. Academic advisors can explain degree and program requirements, policies, and procedures, as well as help you engage in academic planning and problem-solving. They can also refer you to helpful resources throughout the institution. I recommend meeting with an academic advisor at least once each semester. For more on academic advising, see chapter 3.

Counseling Center

Going to college is stressful. There are academic, personal, and social challenges that you will face, and sometimes they may feel unmanageable. The counseling center provides students a confidential, nonthreatening environment in which to explore the issues that pose an obstacle to their academic success and personal well-being. The services provided by the counseling center, either free or for a small charge, may include addressing the following:

- time management
- stress reduction
- test taking
- depression
- anger
- sexual assault
- suicide intervention
- substance abuse
- relationships
- conflict resolution

Career Services

The career services office helps students obtain information about careers. Through a process of self-exploration and career exploration, students can identify career options that will best suit them. Career services may include both career counseling and employment services.

- career testing (interests, values, skills, strengths, personality)
- career information
- employer resources
- internships and cooperative education opportunities

- résumé and cover letter writing
- job search assistance

Technology Support / Computer Labs

Students rely heavily on technology throughout their academic careers. You will be assigned several identities that you will need to remember and use to access services. Typically, you will be assigned a student ID number to use instead of your social security number. This number allows employees to access and review your student records. The second form of identification you will receive is your username. You will use the username for your email and to log in to various resources.

Make note of the information technology help desk number and location. They can help reset passwords and troubleshoot problems with logging in to online courses, uploading documents, and many other needs you may have.

Lack of access to a computer or a last-minute computer crash should not prevent you from submitting assignments on time. Depending on the institution's size, there may be one or multiple computer labs that you can access for free. Find out the labs' hours and locations for quick reference.

Disability Services

Students with documented disabilities can obtain services and accommodations by registering with the disability services office. Accommodations may include extra time on tests, note-takers, wheelchair access, and audio books. The disability services office will notify your professors of your need for accommodations but will not reveal the nature of your disability. If you believe that you may have a learning disability but have not been diagnosed, contact the disability services office to obtain a referral for testing.

Institutions are committed to helping you succeed and provide many services to help you do so. Review your catalog and student handbook, pay attention at orientation, and read the signs around campus to help you discover all that your institution has to offer. You are paying for these services with your tuition, so take advantage of all they have to offer!

CHAPTER 2

Navigating Academic Requirements

2-1 Understanding Degree Requirements

Upon applying to college, you were asked to select a degree and a major. While you may have done some research by reading about the program online or talking with an admissions representative, you may not have a thorough or accurate understanding of what it's all about. Let's dissect a typical undergraduate degree to get a sense of your degree requirements.

Credits

In high school, most courses are assigned either one or a half credit, depending on the content and whether they span the full year or a half year. In college, the assigned credits will depend on two specific factors:

1. The term system the institution is on (semester, quarters)
2. The amount of work required and time spent in class (contact hours)

Traditionally, undergraduate (bachelor) degrees require 120 credits. An associate degree (AA), therefore, requires approximately 60 credits. There are exceptions to these rules based on institutions and programs. You'll have an opportunity to identify and write down your requirements on "My Degree Worksheet" later on in this chapter.

On a traditional semester system, most classes are assigned three credits.

A three-credit course will meet for three hours per week. A typical three-credit course will meet either three days a week for about an hour each time or two times a week for slightly less than an hour and a half each meeting. Evening classes will often meet just once a week for just under three hours.

Courses with content that requires more time to master may have more contact hours and credits. Typically, science, math, and accounting courses may be assigned four credits. Again, this depends entirely on the institution and program. Some programs may assign all of their courses three credits, while others will assign all courses four credits.

Finally, some programs include a few one- and two-credit courses. These courses may be required or optional and include subjects such as freshman seminar, career exploration, physical education, health, and music performance.

Full-Time versus Part-Time Studies

So let's do some math to figure out how many courses you'll be taking each semester and how long it will take you to finish your degree. These calculations are based on a semester-based, four-year degree plan. You may find that your plan will differ, and that's okay. It may take a semester or two to determine whether this plan will work for you or needs to be adjusted. I recommend working closely with an academic advisor to develop an optimal plan for success.

Check with your institution to determine how many credits are considered full-time study. This is an extremely important thing to know for several reasons. Your eligibility for financial aid, as well as the available types and amounts, will depend on whether you are a full- or part-time student. Additionally, you may need to be full-time to be covered by your parents' health insurance or some other benefit. A standard full-time credit load is twelve credits. Some institutions will incentivize students to take more credits each semester by charging a flat tuition rate for up to a certain number of credits (fifteen or eighteen or so). Therefore, it's kind of like a "buy four, get one free" tuition structure.

- Sample rate of progress ÷ Target completion 4 years
- 120 credits ÷ 4 years = 30 credits per year (10 classes per year)

Sample Planning Options

Option 1	Option 2
Fall: 15 credits (5 classes)	Fall: 12 credits (4 classes)
Spring: 15 credits (5 classes)	Spring: 12 credits (4 classes)
Summer: no classes	Summer: 6 credits (2 classes)

What happens if things don't go as planned, though? How far off track will you be if you need to withdraw from a course, fail a course, or need to cut back your credit hours for some other reason?

Scenario:

Pat, eager to get her degree in four years, begins her first semester by enrolling in fifteen credits (she likes the look of option 1, above). As much as she tries, she realizes that she cannot successfully complete all five courses. She withdraws from one of the courses, which she's failing, leaving her to complete twelve credits. So now what? She doesn't fit into either one of the options described above. Should she take eighteen credits in the spring to catch up? Should she plan on taking a course in the summer? I can't say, although I'm never a fan of the "catch up" plan. Pat needs to work with her advisor to find out what makes sense for her.

What's important to understand is that all is not lost just because your plan does not go as expected. You can always reset your goals and academic plan to meet your individual needs and maximize your chances for success!

Degree Components

General Education

To help you become a well-rounded student (and, ultimately, employee) who can think critically, analyze problems, develop creative solutions, and communicate effectively, colleges have developed a strategic framework that is intended to expose you to a variety of subjects. This framework is called "general education." The general education framework is distributed among several disciplines, typically in areas such as the following:

- English composition and literature
- communications
- mathematics
- science
- social and behavioral sciences
- humanities

Additional requirements may also be part of the general education framework that are intended to build specific competencies, such as writing, or ensure exposure to certain concepts, such as cultural awareness. The number of credits dedicated to general education courses may vary, but the average is around thirty-six credits (twelve classes).

Navigating general education requirements can be difficult. The requirements, which can be found in the catalog or online curriculum, are often listed with notes and criteria that must be satisfied. I strongly recommend that you frequently refer to the general education requirements and consult with an academic advisor to make sure that you're on track with general education requirements.

Below is an example of the notes and references you may find when reviewing curricular requirements. As you can see, they can be quite confusing. When reviewing your curriculum, read carefully, understand the notes, and work with an academic advisor so that you learn what is required of you.

Sample General Education Excerpt

Satisfactorily complete one course in each of the twelve numbered areas.			**36 hours**
A. Communications			9 hours
1.	ENG 101	Composition I [1, 2, 3]	3(3,0)
2.	ENG 102	Composition II Prereq: ENG 101 [1, 2]	3(3,0)
3.	SPC 101L	Fundamentals of Speech [a]	3(3,0)
	COM 100	Introduction to Communication [b]	3(3,0)

Students have the option to pursue a 24-semester-credit specialized program by completing ENG 226, or ENG 226H or SPC 300, or SPC 300H, and ORI 101 or ORI 101H and the six-semester-credit mathematics requirement outlined in Area 5. See "specialized program" section for more information.

Major Requirements

Major requirements are the courses that are specialized based on your area of interest or intended career. The number of credits devoted to your major will vary depending on what major you pursue. Some majors are highly prescriptive—that is, made up of a very specific set of courses. Business, mathematics, and health sciences are examples of highly prescribed majors. Other majors are more flexible and provide you more choices regarding which courses you take. Liberal arts and the social sciences (psychology, sociology) may give you more options or tracks that you can follow.

Generally, you will begin taking major courses in your sophomore year and continue to take more of them in your junior and senior years. A lot of this will depend on what your major is and how many prerequisites and specific course sequences you need (we'll get to that in a minute). You may want to take some major courses in your freshman year, as well. It's especially a good idea if you want to "try out" content to see if you like it and also a good way to stay interested if you're not particularly thrilled about your general education courses. If you take several major courses and decide that major is not right for you, most likely you'll be able to use them as electives (see below).

You can determine which major courses are meant to be taken in which year by the course numbering system. A rule of thumb is if the course number begins with a 1, it is an introductory course and is okay to take in your freshman year (e.g., ENG 101 or MAT 1100). If it begins with a 2, it is meant for your sophomore year, 3 is for your junior year, and 4 is for your senior year. Please note that this is a broad generalization that is not set in stone. More commonly, courses are broken down into *lower division* and *upper division* courses. Lower division courses are numbered 100–299 (or 1000–2999, depending on the institution's system), while upper division courses are numbered 300–499 or 3000–4999.

Electives

Most undergraduate majors have room for at least a few elective courses. Electives are courses that can be categorized in almost any discipline or academic level. There are usually some restrictions on electives. Typically, they need to be college-level (not preparatory or developmental level) courses and cannot be from a career-track program such as dental hygiene or construction. Look to your catalog or advisor to provide you a list of viable elective courses.

Electives are a great way to explore subjects that you might be interested in as well as rule out those that you don't want to pursue. Electives are also good for supplementing your own personal and professional development. Some great ways to constructively use electives are to take a freshman seminar (may be called student success or something similar) or a career exploration course. Internships are also a highly valuable way to strategically use your electives, as employment opportunities often arise from student internships.

For majors that have very prescribed course sequences that include a series of prerequisites (I promise, I'll get to that soon), elective slots are often used up by the prescribed prerequisite courses, leaving little or no flexibility in this area.

Minors

Minors are made up of a set of courses that focus on a secondary discipline area. Instead of taking general elective courses, students who choose to add a minor take very specific courses in a subject area. You do not earn a minor by simply taking the prescribed courses. A minor must be formally requested and added to your record. Check your catalog for the procedure for declaring a minor, as the rules and procedures will vary from college to college.

Students often ask if a minor is important or if it "looks good" to an employer or graduate school. It's a hard question to answer. Think of it like this—if you have a major in business and a minor in psychology, you are telling an employer, "I know a lot about business and also psychology." If you are hoping to go into management, human resources, or organizational behavior, this combination might help to sell you as a qualified candidate. However, a minor is in no way required or expected in most circumstances. I generally recommend minors to students who are either torn between two subject areas and want to study both or want to learn a lot about a second academic discipline. You most likely will have time to decide if you want to pursue a minor. In fact, some programs don't let you apply for one until your sophomore year or later.

Prerequisites/Corequisites

Within your degree program, you can expect to encounter courses that have prerequisites or corequisites. Prerequisites are courses that are required before taking other courses, while corequisites are courses that are required to be taken at the same time. Below are some common examples of pre- and corequisites.

Prerequisite course sequences:

- English Composition I → English Composition II → Literature
- Intermediate algebra → Algebra I → Precalculus → Calculus

Corequisite courses:

- Biology + Biology Lab
- Chemistry + Chemistry Lab

Some majors require very specific course sequences that must be followed carefully in order to satisfy degree requirements or prepare for entry into a major. As you engage in academic planning, make sure to take these prerequisites into account so that you can stay on track. Two popular majors that are notorious for strict course sequences are business administration (more math than you might think) and nursing (lots of science).

Below you will find a diagram illustrating the traditional four-year completion sequence for a bachelor's degree and the types of courses you will be taking each year.

The Structure of a Bachelor's Degree

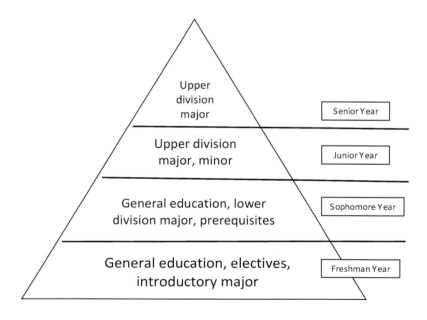

My Degree Worksheet

Complete the following worksheet and keep a copy for your reference. Use the university, department, and program websites, along with the catalog, to complete the worksheet. Make sure to review the worksheet with your academic advisor to ensure completeness and accuracy.

My institution uses a   ☐ semester   ☐ quarter   ☐ other   calendar

Are there half or partial semesters?   ☐ yes   ☐ no

To be a full-time student,
I must enroll in   ___credits each   ☐ semester   ☐ quarter   ☐ other: __

There   ☐ is ☐ is not   a flat tuition structure.   I can take up to ___ credits for one tuition price

My degree is _____ and requires _____ credits

My major is _____

General education is made up of __ credits   The general education areas are:

Area _____   _____ credits

Area _____   _____ credits

Area _____   _____ credits

Area _____   _____ credits

Area _____   _____ credits

Area _____   _____ credits

The major requires   _____ credits

The electives require   _____ credits

The minor (optional) requires   _____ credits

What areas have course sequences (prerequisites)?   ☐   English

                                                   ☐   Mathematics

                                                   ☐   Science

                                                   ☐   Other

Tools and Resources

There's a lot to keep track of when pursuing your degree. How do you know that you're taking the right courses and haven't missed anything? As I've mentioned, your academic advisor will be a great source of information. I'll discuss more about the advising process and relationship in chapter 3. However, it is ultimately up to you to understand and complete your degree requirements. Even if it is tempting to claim, "Nobody told me" or "I couldn't find it," you will be held responsible for completing all degree requirements.

Degree Audit

Most institutions have an electronic degree audit in place for students to access degree requirements and monitor their progress toward degree completion. Each institution may call it something different, so make sure to specifically ask, "Where can I find my degree audit?" It might be called something cute that ties into the school's brand, like "Tiger Tracker," or it might be hidden in some acronym with which you are unfamiliar, such as DRS (Degree Requirement System).

A degree audit outlines the exact requirements of your specific program based on your catalog year or term. Even if the degree requirements change for future students, your catalog year or term will determine what courses you will be required to take. As you successfully complete courses and meet criteria for degree completion, your degree audit will reflect your progress by filling in the requirement with the course and grade. Some degree audits use a color-coded system wherein green means a requirement has been met and red means it has not. Other audits use a "yes/no" system, where yes means it is complete and no means it is not. You may even see the terms *met* and *unmet*. It's important that you become familiar with how to read your degree audit so that you know exactly what's required of you.

How to Read Your Degree Audit

Generally, a degree audit will include the following sections:

- Degree requirements:
  - o Required credits to complete
  - o Minimum GPA (Grade Point Average): The minimum GPA that is required to graduate
  - o Program/Major GPA: You may need to have a higher GPA in your major courses than your overall GPA
- Areas: General education, major, minor, and electives usually are broken down into separate sections
- Criteria and conditions: Requirements such as a minimum acceptable grade for a course or a writing requirement will often be included in the degree audit

The bottom line is that when you have completed all the degree requirements, everything should be green, say *met*, or have everything marked with a *yes*. Pay attention to anything that is not marked as completed. The first couple of times that you access your degree audit, be prepared to be confused at first. Then, take a breath and read each section carefully. Make a note of anything you don't understand and ask your academic advisor. The following is an example of an excerpt from a degree audit.

Sample Excerpt from Degree Audit
(notes added for clarification)

Overall GPA	2.0	2.75	Yes
Program GPA	2.5	0.0	No

Notes:
- *Student's GPA is higher than minimum*
- *Student has not taken any major courses so does not have program GPA*

Area 1: Composition and Communication (9 cr)   Not Met
Students must earn a C or better in the following courses:

ENG 101	Introduction to Composition	B	Yes
ENG 102	Introduction to Literature	C–	No
SPC 100			No

Notes:
- *Student has not successfully passed all three courses*
- *Student has not met minimum grade requirement*
- *Course may not appear if it has not been taken*

Area 2: Mathematics (6 cr)   Not Met
Students must have two college-level courses at the college algebra level or higher:

MAT 111	No
Choose from the following: MAT 200, 211, 321, 342	No

Area 3: Social and Behavioral Sciences (6 cr)   Not Met
Must have one global awareness course

PSY 101	Introduction to Psychology	A	Yes
PSY 102	Abnormal Psychology	B	Yes

Notes:
- *Neither PSY 101 nor 102 is a global awareness course*

Area 5: Electives   **(24 cr)**   Not Met

ENG 102	Introduction to Literature	C–
MAT 101	Introduction to Algebra	A

Notes:
- *Student has not completed required number of credits*
- *Courses that do not meet other requirements may appear here*
- *MAT 101 is a credit course but does not satisfy the math requirement*

2-2 Understanding Academic Standing

Let's face it—not all students are straight-A students. In fact, most are probably not. You will encounter subjects that are interesting to you and some courses that are easier for you to master than others. As a result, there may be times that earning an A seems relatively effortless, while other times, pulling off a passing grade can seem almost impossible. As you have already experienced in high school, your knowledge, abilities, focus, attitude, and behaviors all directly contribute to your success—or lack thereof—in school. In college, your academic progress will be closely monitored, and D and F grades may put you at risk of being suspended or dismissed from the program. Any courses that you attempt but do not complete may also jeopardize your eligibility for financial aid.

Grade Point Average (GPA)

As you go through your program and earn grades, those grades will be calculated into your GPA. This GPA will determine your academic standing, and if it does not meet the set standards, it can jeopardize your ability to continue your studies. A low GPA can also negatively impact your eligibility for financial aid.

There are typically three types of GPAs. The first is your overall GPA, also known as the cumulative GPA. You may find it on your transcript under the notation "cum GPA." The cumulative GPA calculates all of your grades and is used to determine eligibility for graduation, financial aid, and academic standing. The second type of GPA is a program or major GPA. The program or major GPA is determined by calculating the grades earned in the required courses for your major (for instance, your psychology courses if you're a psychology major). In general, program or major GPA standards may be higher than the overall GPA. You may find that the overall GPA requirement is 2.0 but the major GPA requirement is 2.25. If you earned straight Cs in your psychology courses, your major GPA would not meet minimum standards since straight Cs would result in a 2.0 GPA. Finally, your semester GPA will reflect your progress for an individual semester. This calculation will be important should you find yourself on academic warning or probation.

Academic Standing

Academic programs and degrees have set standards to measure success. A common standard for undergraduate students is a minimum GPA of 2.0 (C average). If you meet the minimum required GPA, you are considered in "good standing." If you fall below the required standard, you will be placed in a different academic standing until you raise your GPA to the minimum acceptable standard. Your academic standing will be determined based on your GPA, length in the program, and progress toward improvement. Students who encounter academic difficulty for the first time may be placed on academic warning or probation to catch their attention and provide intervention for success. If your GPA continues to fall below the set standards, you may be at risk for suspension or dismissal.

Calculating Your GPA

The institution will automatically calculate your GPA every semester, and it will appear on your transcript and other records such as your degree audit. However, I recommend understanding how GPA is calculated and checking your transcript each semester to verify that your GPA is accurately noted. Occasionally, a mistake can occur on your records, resulting in an inaccurate GPA. By knowing and understanding how to calculate your GPA, you can ensure that your records are accurate. You can also figure out what future grades you need to earn in order to raise your GPA. Below is the standard format for calculating GPA. Make sure to find out how your institution calculates GPA in case it differs from the example below. You can usually find GPA calculations in the catalog. Additionally, there are lots of wonderful, easy-to-use GPA calculators online that can help you with questions such as "If I earn an A in this class, what will my GPA be?" or "What grades do I need to earn this semester to return to good standing?" You may find that your institution has its own GPA calculator for you to use.

The following factors are involved in calculating your GPA:

- credits completed
- grade points
- quality points

Sample GPA Calculation

The first thing you'll want to know is the point value for each assigned grade. You can find the grading scale in course syllabi and the college catalog. Below is a simple, standard scale, but your institution may use a different grading scale.

A	=	4.0
B+	=	3.5
B	=	3.0
C+	=	2.5
C	=	2.0
D+	=	1.5
D	=	1.0
F	=	0.0

Course	Grade		Points		Credits		Quality Points (QP)
PSY 101	A	=	4.0	x	3.0	=	12
ENG 101	B+	=	3.5	x	3.0	=	10.5
ORI 100	A	=	4.0	x	3.0	=	12
MAT 101	C	=	2.0	x	3.0	=	6
Totals					**12**		**40.5**

GPA = Quality Points (QP) ÷ Total Credits: 40.5 ÷ 12 = **3.375** (might round to 3.38 or 3.4)

In this example, the student's semester GPA is 3.375. If this is a first-semester student, his or her overall GPA is also 3.375.

What if this student wants to know what grades he or she will need the following semester in order to reach a 3.5 GPA? The same formula is used, tallying up all grades earned plus projected grades. It is important to note that you cannot average each semester to find your overall GPA (e.g., 3.5 fall semester + 4.0 spring semester = 7.5 ÷ 2 semesters *does not equal* your GPA).

Course	Grade		Points		Credits		Quality Points (QP)
Spring							
PSY 101	A	=	4.0	x	3.0	=	12
ENG 101	B+	=	3.5	x	3.0	=	10.5
ORI 100	A	=	4.0	x	3.0	=	12
MAT 101	C	=	2.0	x	3.0	=	6
Summer	What if I earned a …						
BIO 110	B	=	3.0	x	4.0	=	12
Totals					16		52.5
	52.5 ÷ 16 = **3.28**						
OR	What if I earned an …						
BIO 110	A	=	4.0	x	4.0	=	16
Totals					16		56.5
	56.5 ÷ 16 = **3.53**						

In this example, if the student earns an A for the summer term, the semester GPA for the summer will be a 4.0 and the overall GPA will be a 3.53. An earned A will raise the overall GPA to the desired 3.5. A grade of B would lower the overall GPA.

If you are not a fan of math or numbers, this calculation may seem intimidating. However, once you apply the simple calculations, it will not be so overwhelming.

GPA Calculation Formula								
Semester	Course	Grade		Points		Credits		Quality Points (QP)
	Course:		=		x		=	
	Course:		=		x		=	
	Course:		=		x		=	
	Course:		=		x		=	
	Course:		=		x		=	
	Course:		=		x		=	
	Course:		=		x		=	
	Course:		=		x		=	
	Course:		=		x		=	
	Course:		=		x		=	
	Totals					Total Credits:		Total Quality Points:
				Overall, cumulative GPA:				Total Quality Points ÷ Total Credits =

Notes:

We establish academic guidelines and standards to ensure that you are satisfactorily learning assigned material that will lead to your overall success. While the monitoring of academic progress may feel punitive, the system is designed to help students remain enrolled, rather than leave. Most institutions and departments have some form of intervention to support academically at-risk students. If you find yourself out of good standing, make sure to seek help from an academic advisor or student success specialist to develop a plan to improve your standing.

Early Warning Program

Some institutions and departments may use an early warning program to alert students to potential risks to their academic standing. A student who does not display behaviors that are consistent with academic success may be identified by a professor and referred to an early intervention program to help the student avoid poor or failing grades. Some red flags that may indicate academic difficulty include poor attendance, lateness, failure to submit assignments, lack of participation, or low grades. If you find yourself exhibiting these behaviors or experiencing these challenges, I encourage you to seek assistance from an academic advisor or student support professional. If you are given an opportunity to receive additional services and support, take it! These programs are designed to help you avoid getting into academic difficulty and are a great way to do so. Services may include referral to tutoring, study skills workshops, stress-management workshops, and writing support.

Academic Warning

It is natural that new students may experience a shift in academic rigor from high school to college. Other factors, such as homesickness and adjustment issues, might also affect your academic performance.

During your first semester or year, should your GPA fall below satisfactory standards, you may be placed on academic warning. Academic warning is usually a wake-up call that is intended to let you know that your grades are not sufficient to remain in good standing. It is like a warning light in a car that alerts you to potential problems. Think of a tire indicator. If it comes on, you know that you need to do something (add air to the tires) to avoid a flat tire. If you do not do anything when the indicator comes on, you may, indeed, end up with a flat tire. Academic warning is an indicator that something is wrong and needs to be addressed. You may need help in test-taking, writing, managing your time, getting tutoring, or managing stress. Get the help you need early to avoid more serious consequences. Without intervention or change, you may find yourself stranded on the side of the road with four flat tires.

Academic Probation

Academic probation is often the second tier of academic standing. Students who have been placed on academic warning (if the institution uses a warning system) and fail to achieve the acceptable GPA required to return to good standing may be placed on academic probation. This is a more serious warning indicator for you. Students placed on academic probation will be provided a specific set of criteria that must be met in order to return to good academic standing. Students who are on academic probation and fail to achieve the necessary GPA for good standing may be suspended from the program or institution.

Many institutions offer programs and support for students who are on academic probation. Whether mandatory or voluntary, I highly recommend participating in any probation intervention programs that your institution offers should you find yourself on academic probation.

Academic Suspension

Students who have been placed on academic probation and do not meet the standards outlined in their terms of probation are at risk for academic suspension. Students who are placed on academic suspension are prohibited from taking classes for a set duration of time. Specific criteria must also be met before students are allowed to resume studies. Students who are on academic suspension may find that they are not allowed to take courses within other programs or institutions, so it is important to understand the consequences of being placed on academic suspension, as well as the criteria for reentering the institution. If you are suspended, make sure to connect with student support resources and personnel so that you can maximize your chances for a successful reentry.

Academic Dismissal

Institutions often allow students who have been suspended to resume their studies under a specific set of criteria and expectations. Students who do not meet those expectations are at risk for academic dismissal. Since students who return from suspension are given a second chance to be successful in their programs, it is essential that they achieve academic success upon reentry. If they do not, the institution may dismiss them. Academic dismissal is final and permanent. Students who are academically dismissed may not return to their programs—and possibly their institutions—and may have difficulty being accepted into other programs or institutions.

Academic Progress

You will be monitored for academic progress throughout your program—that is, whether you are earning satisfactory grades and completing courses at a reasonable pace. In addition to using grades as an indicator for progress, institutions may also look at credits attempted versus credits earned and the number of dropped or withdrawn courses. Lack of academic progress may result in any of the above academic standings but also may result in the loss of eligibility for financial aid. Make sure to learn what criteria are used to determine whether you are making satisfactory academic progress.

Strategies for Achieving Academic Success

There are many reasons a student might struggle and find that he or she has been placed on academic warning or probation. Lack of dedicated study time, heavy course load, poor writing skills, difficulty in test taking, or inability to master course content may all jeopardize a student's academic standing.

As you engage in academic planning, consider the following:

- Do I have enough time to study for all the classes in which I'm registered?
- Are any of the subjects that I'm taking difficult for me? If so, which ones?

- Are there other time commitments and activities that might get in the way of my academic success? If so, which ones? Which activities can I give up, if necessary?
- Do I get nervous on tests and forget everything I know?
- Is there stress in my life that gets in the way of my concentration and studying?
- What areas do I need to strengthen? Math? Writing?
- Do I have a balanced schedule that includes challenging courses and courses that come easier to me?
- Are my social activities preventing me from sleeping and studying adequately?

The best way to meet academic expectations is to be proactive (i.e., "What do I need to do to achieve academic success?") rather than reactive ("What do I need to do to get back in good academic standing?"). By establishing productive relationships with your academic advisor and other student support personnel, you can develop positive habits early on to minimize the risk of academic difficulty.

Academic Progress Standards and Strategies Checklist

Check all the academic standing designations your institution uses:

- ☐ Academic warning
- ☐ Academic probation
- ☐ Academic suspension
- ☐ Academic dismissal
- ☐ Other: _____

I must maintain a _____ cumulative GPA to remain in good standing with the institution.

I ☐ do ☐ do not have to meet a minimum GPA for my specific academic program. If yes, what is the minimum acceptable GPA? _____

If my GPA falls below _____, I will be placed on academic warning.

To get back into good standing after being placed on academic warning, I must _____.

If my GPA falls below _____, I will be placed on academic probation.

To get back into good standing after being placed on academic probation, I must _____.

If my GPA falls below _____, I will be placed on academic suspension.

To get back into good standing after being placed on academic suspension, I must _____.

Notes:

_____

_____

_____

_____

_____

_____

Grading Scale and Quality Points

Check the grades that are offered at your institution, as well as the corresponding quality points for each grade. Please note that not all institutions have a plus/minus system.

	Grade	Quality Points
	Example	
	A	4.0
	A–	3.7
☐	A	
☐	A–	
☐	B+	
☐	B	
☐	B–	
☐	C+	
☐	C	
☐	C–	
☐	D+	
☐	D	
☐	D–	
☐	F	

Questions to Ask about Academic Standards

What support services are available to me if I am placed on:

Early warning? _____

_____

Academic warning? _____

_____

Academic probation? _____

_____

Academic suspension? _____

_____

What strategies do you suggest for me to return to satisfactory academic standing?

_____

_____

_____

_____

What is expected of me if I am placed on:

Early warning? _____

_____

Academic warning? _____

_____

Academic probation? _____

_____

Academic suspension? _____

_____

2-3 Online Courses

Throughout your college career, you very likely may be required to take, or want to take, an online course. While online courses are a great option for those who want the flexibility and independence that come with studying online, they can be challenging for students who tend to procrastinate or who are not skilled in self-management. Let's look at some of the myths surrounding online courses and explore the reality of the online experience.

Myths

Online Courses Are Easier

It depends on what you mean by *easier*. Yes, it is convenient that you don't have to schlep across campus to get to class on time or worry about whether you're going to have to sit way in the back or right up front. The idea of "going to class" in your pj's might be quite appealing. However, a common myth is that online courses require less work since there are no actual class sessions to attend.

It's important to know that when they are developing curriculum, academic departments must adhere to the same course requirements and standards for their online courses as their classroom-based courses. Therefore, you need to achieve the same learning outcomes whether you're sitting in front of the professor or your laptop.

When you first enter an online course, it can be scary. Unlike face-to-face classes, everything may be preloaded into the course the same day. Each assignment, discussion post, and project, with detailed descriptions, may be available for your review right from the start, which can be overwhelming. However, you might find that some professors choose to upload content throughout the semester, which is more like a classroom-based course.

Online courses are primarily asynchronous, meaning that there is minimal live interaction between students and the professor. Most of the work is made available to students upon entering the course, along with due dates for assignments and projects. You'll be responsible for meeting those deadlines. While you may receive some written reminders from the professor, generally, you will be responsible for setting your own reminders regarding due dates and deadlines.

Despite the common myth that online courses are easier than their classroom counterparts, many students find them to be more difficult. The two main reasons for that are the amount of independent work and self-discipline that are required in online courses and the amount of extra time that is built into an online course to compensate for the three hours per week that are normally spent in a classroom. Since there are no class meeting times, it is expected that you will work on your course for those three hours each week in addition to the normal amount of time you need to study and complete assignments.

It's Easier to Cheat in an Online Course

Online course delivery varies from institution to institution. Each college and department may have different ways to monitor academic dishonesty. Professors who teach online are experienced professionals and are skilled at spotting plagiarism and cheating. Some institutions use online platforms that allow students to be visually monitored as they take tests and other systems to verify that students are doing their own work.

In my experience as an online professor, it is easier to identify instances of dishonesty and cheating in an online course. If you're in my classroom and say something, I cannot quickly refer to other sources to make sure you are using your own words. I must trust that you are. However, in an online environment, I can use resources such as TurnItIn ® or a simple Google ® search to spot instances of plagiarism. I urge you to avoid cheating or plagiarizing in an online course and, instead, enjoy the flexibility and self-direction that the online environment provides.

You Can Set Your Own Pace in an Online Course

The asynchronous nature of online courses does not mean that you can do your work whenever you want and that, if you need a little more time, you'll have it. *Asynchronous* only means that communication between students and the professor (or among students) is not live. You submit your work or questions and receive feedback later. While some institutions are implementing flex programs that do allow you to complete courses at your own pace, most online courses follow a traditional semester or quarter system.

To be successful in an online course, make sure to add dates and deadlines to your calendar. As with all courses, I recommend budgeting a few days between when you complete the work and when it is due. This helps to create a cushion should anything come up that prevents you from doing your work. The number one excuse I receive about late work is that the student had "technology problems." Power failure, hardware glitches, lack of Internet, or poor Internet service are all reasons students might have for missing a deadline. By working ahead, you'll have a few days to solve these problems if you encounter them or at least get to a public computer to submit your work.

Online courses may be set up to restrict submission of late work. In fact, the assignment may "go away" and no longer be visible after the due date, or the system may block you from submitting work even if you can see the assignment. Also, grading for late or missed work may be immediate, as it can be configured in the online course structure. So if you're used to using your best, most winning and cute smile to talk the professor into accepting a late assignment, you may be in for a shock in an online environment.

The Professors Do Not Teach in an Online Course

I've heard students complain that online learning is nothing more than teaching themselves the material. "Why have a professor at all?" some have wondered. It's important to be aware that the professor spends a lot of time and energy developing course content; creating lectures, assignments, and activities; as well as providing you resources that will help you learn the material. In the online world, this is teaching. It feels different only because it is asynchronous. If a classroom professor says, "Pull out your textbook and look at chapter 4," it is considered acceptable teaching practice. If that same professor in an online environment says, "Read chapter 4 and summarize the main points," it is easier to discount that as teaching. Take advantage of all the resources and information that the professor provides in class.

Just because a professor is not standing in front of you, it does not mean that he or she is not available to speak with or is uninterested in getting to know you. I recommend trying to get to know your professor and interacting with him or her. Just as with the student experience, online teaching can be a bit of a lonely experience. Professors who teach online are eager to engage with their students and are available for phone and possibly face-to-face appointments.

You Can Avoid Group Projects in an Online Course

Nope. If online coursework is attractive to you so you can avoid those frustrating group projects, you will be greatly disappointed. In fact, online courses often have more group work than classroom courses, simply because it is a good way to get students to engage with one another. In a classroom, you walk in, take a seat next to someone, and eventually strike up a conversation. Your online course professor knows the importance of student connections and interactions and will attempt to facilitate those connections through different means. Group projects are one way to get you thinking and talking about the course content, as well as to take responsibility for your learning.

Group projects can be difficult, both from the professor's and student's viewpoint. Inevitably, someone doesn't participate. Some students aren't available to meet. Other students submit plagiarized or poor-quality work, and you're being graded on it. Hang in there. The best way to face challenges in a group project is to take responsibility for your own work and take leadership in convening meetings or moving things along. Just as with face-to-face group work, make sure that each member has a role and that each member's work can be clearly identified. While many students feel that it is not fair that they "always" have to take a leadership role in group work, it is the best way to ensure that you will get the grade you deserve.

Online Course Structure

Below are the main parts of an online course. When you log in to your course for the first time, take note of the parts and how to navigate the course.

Chats

Chats are synchronous in nature—that is, a time is set for all students and the professor to meet and talk. Types of chats may include a lecture on a course topic, as well as student class presentations. Communication within a chat could be done in a variety of ways. The professor may speak into a microphone, but your microphone might be muted. Other times, both the students and the professor have speaking ability. A typed chat feature is used in some courses, wherein you can type in your questions and answers. Chats may be recorded for those students who can't make it, and presentation materials may be made available after the chat. Make sure to mark down the dates for chats, and as with a classroom-based course, arrive on time and participate when prompted. This is one of the few opportunities to talk with your professor and classmates, so take advantage!

Discussion Posts

Online courses frequently include a discussion post section. Discussion posts allow students to research and reflect on a topic and then share their thoughts with both the professor and their peers. It is the closest thing to having a class discussion on a topic in a classroom environment. Most likely, you will be required to respond to a discussion post prompt on a weekly basis, as well as respond to other peers' postings. Think of it as sitting next to one another in class. Rather than saying, "I agree with what you just said," make a point to further the discussion. Just as it would be kind of awkward to tell someone you agree without saying why, responding to a peer's post with such a statement is weak and does not move the discussion forward. Your professor is trying to replicate discussion with these posts, and you'll get more out of it if you remind yourself that is the point.

Assignments

The assignments area of the course will include any tests or assignments you have for class. This is where you will find the assignment topics, grading weight, and due dates. Assignments might be individual or may include group work.

Lectures

Some professors may include weekly or frequent lectures. These lectures might come in the form of prerecorded presentations with slides and audio, while others may be written only. Another type of lecture is a recorded video of a classroom lecture. Make sure to keep up with any lectures that are available. Missing these lectures will be as disadvantageous as missing a live class session.

Announcements

In most face-to-face classes, the professor starts the class with a few announcements, and he or she most likely will end the class with a few more. For online courses, the professor uses the announcements function to replicate that feature of classroom teaching. The professor may set up the announcements for you to read on your own or may arrange for the announcements to be sent to your class or university email. Each system is a bit different, so find out where these announcements are going so you won't miss one. Announcements might include important changes to the course, reminders of deadlines, or helpful supplemental resources. If you don't receive announcements in email, make it a practice to check the announcements section once a day.

Email

You should never feel isolated from your professor. Your professor is available to talk with you via phone, in person (if local), or by email. One of the most commonly used methods of communicating in an online course is via course email. This feature is embedded in the online course and is often separate from your university email. It is important to know how your professor wants to communicate with you. When he or she asks you to send an email, ask if he or she prefers that you to send it via course email or university email. It can be frustrating for both students and professors when they are sending emails back and forth to different accounts. In general, students should use the course email to communicate with the professor and other students. The professor will tell you if that is not the preferred method of communication.

Tips for a Successful Online Course Experience

- Even if it is not a requirement, take at least one online course. If nothing else, it will be a unique learning experience for you. It will also help you prepare for future online study, especially in graduate school.
- If there is not a defined period in which you must take an online course, wait until you are ready. Become established as a successful college student before attempting an online course. I recommend no sooner than your second (sophomore) year, but the more experienced and mature you are, the more likely you'll have success in an online course.
- Learn how to navigate the course right from the start. Click away! Explore every link that's in the course. You'll be surprised at how much information and how many resources are available in an online course.
- Establish relationships. Just as with a classroom-based course, your experience will be better if you have at least one student with whom you can chat and exchange ideas. Similarly, get to know your professor, and become more than just a name to him or her.
- Develop systems for meeting deadlines, reading, and doing research. The asynchronous nature of online courses may throw you a bit, and it's easy to get behind.

If, after taking an online course, you find that you like the format, take more. Just be sure to avoid isolating yourself as a result. It is important to actively establish yourself as part of your institution's community. As you take online courses, you risk missing out on the socialization and relationship-building that is an important part of college life. Keep going to events; joining clubs; hanging out in common areas such as residence halls or the student center; and engaging with staff, faculty, and students to maximize your college experience.

CHAPTER 3

GETTING WHAT YOU NEED
WHEN YOU NEED IT

3-1 Let Your Advisor Be Your Lifeline

After having spent most of my career as an academic advisor, I'd like to believe that advisors are the most important resource within the college setting. While there are wonderfully supportive and helpful personnel throughout the institution who can help you, your academic advisor can serve as the focal point for providing consistent, ongoing support and direction to you throughout your academic career. Upon entering college, make sure to find out who your advisor is and where he or she is located. Although that sounds easy enough, it might be harder than you think depending on the advising model that your institution has. Let's look at a few types of advising models and terminology related to academic advising.

What Academic Advising Is and Why It's Important

The first thing I want to stress is the importance of obtaining early and ongoing academic advising. I recommend meeting with an advisor after you've been admitted and before you register for your first semester. Many institutions will have a formal process for introducing new students to advising and initiating the first registration. However, if you do not hear from an advisor shortly after being admitted, reach out and inquire as to how you can make an advising appointment. Then, make sure to meet with an advisor a minimum of once a semester.

In the academic advising session, you can expect to discuss several topics, including

- your major, how and why you chose it (new students), or how you like it (continuing students);
- career goals;
- placement in math and English courses;
- overview of curriculum;
- academic planning and course selection for the upcoming term;
- academic experience—successes and challenges;
- progress toward degree completion;
- referral to resources; and
- questions or concerns you may have.

Even if you have carefully reviewed the catalog and degree audit, it is important to verify with an advisor that you are on the right track, as well as discuss your academic plan and any obstacles you've experienced or anticipate. An academic advisor is your advocate and is a valuable source of support and information. Too many times, upon meeting a student late in his or her program and after experiencing a problem, I have heard the student exclaim, "I wish I had met you earlier! I could have avoided all these problems." Don't have any regrets. Line up your resources early, and they will be there when you need them.

Types of Advisors

Several types of advisors may be involved in providing you academic advising. You may be assigned a specific advisor or be able to access one of several advisors. Advisors may be systematically assigned by student last name or academic level or may be assigned by college or major. Find out if you will be assigned a specific advisor and, if so, who it is. If your institution does not assign advisors, try to establish a relationship with one or two good advisors. If you do not have an assigned advisor, it is okay to ask for a specific individual and build a rapport with that person. For departments that don't have assigned advisors, more popular advisors may be requested more frequently, which may cause a delay in service. That's why it's a good idea to have a few advisors on whom you can rely. If you do not meet with the same advisor each time, make sure to keep personal notes about your advising sessions as well as the options discussed and decisions that were made. Feel free to ask your advisor if he or she has access to notes about your previous advising session or if he or she would like you to summarize what took place. By doing so, you can bring the new advisor up to speed about where you are and what you are thinking.

Professional Academic Advisor

Professional academic advisors generally work full-time in the advising field. The primary duty of a professional advisor is to provide individual and group advising to students. These advisors are well versed in degree requirements, including general education, majors, minors, and electives. Professional advisors are also very experienced with institutional and college-specific policies and procedures. They are often responsible for verifying that students have met all requirements for degree conferral. In addition to their knowledge about academic requirements, policies, and procedures, professional academic advisors are also knowledgeable about valuable resources and services throughout the institution, such as tutoring, student activities, disability services, and student support services.

Faculty Advisor

Faculty advisors are housed within academic departments and are subject-matter experts in the areas in which they teach. Some institutions use a faculty advising model to connect students with faculty who share similar academic and professional goals. Faculty advisors are skilled at discussing the content of major courses and curriculum. Institutions with faculty advising models may also have a separate student services department or unit that assists students in dropping and adding courses, testing, and many of the administrative functions of professional advisors. The primary role of faculty advisors is to teach, but they usually have additional responsibilities in research and service to the community. Faculty advisors generally have fewer advisees than professional advisors, which provides an opportunity for relationship building.

Sue Ohrablo, Ed.D.

Peer Advisor

Peer advisors are students who can provide information and direction regarding curricular requirements, policies and procedures, and referral to resources. The benefit of speaking to a peer advisor is that these students have "been through it" and can provide you a student's perspective on navigating college. Be careful to listen for bias, however, because when seeking advising, you need facts, not opinions. Peer advisors are usually trained and supervised by professional advisors and are used to help alleviate student traffic and answer commonly asked questions.

Types of Advising Offices

Now that you have a better understanding of who will be providing you advising, it's important to find out where they may be located.

Academic Advising Center

In smaller colleges, there may be one central advising department or center. This center can often be found in a building that houses student-support types of functions such as financial aid, counseling, and the registrar's office. In larger institutions, such as universities, there may be more than one academic advising center. These centers may be housed within colleges (such as the college of business advising center) or departments (such as the accounting advising center).Within some institutions, you can obtain academic advising from the same department throughout your entire program. However, some institutions have a model wherein you begin with a freshman or general advisor and then are transitioned to a faculty advisor, commonly in your sophomore or junior year.

Faculty Advising Offices

Faculty advisors are generally located in an academic department among their faculty peers. For instance, if you go to the psychology department, all or many of the psychology faculty will be located there. This is where you will find your faculty advisor. Since faculty advisors have multiple responsibilities, advising will most likely occur in the faculty member's office.

Types of Academic Advising Sessions

Advising can be delivered in many ways. Find out what your options are regarding receiving advising. While some advising departments provide a variety of delivery methods for advising, some may not. By knowing how advising is delivered, you can reduce frustration that may result from inappropriate expectations.

Appointments

If appointments are available, I highly recommend making at least one appointment with your advisor each semester. Appointments provide you a dedicated time with your advisor, generally in a half- or full-hour block of time, during which you can engage in discussion about academic planning and ask any questions you may have. Both you and the advisor can focus on your success without distractions from other students who are waiting or phones that are ringing.

Face-to-Face

Face-to-face appointments are usually held in an advisor's office within an advising center or in a faculty advisor's office. Depending on the comfort level of the student and advisor, departmental policy, and need for privacy, the door may be kept open or closed. Face-to-face appointments are a great way to build a relationship with an advisor.

Web Conference

Students who attend in an online or multicampus environment may not be able to meet with an advisor in person. The next best thing to a face-to-face, in-person advising session is web-conferencing. If the institution provides this option, you can benefit from meeting your advisor via a web-based service such as

Skype ®, Zoom ®, or GoToMeeting ®. Web advising is a step above phone or email as it gives you a chance to see each other, therefore making it easier to get to know each other as individuals. With a screen-share feature, advisors can navigate websites and resources with students, and students can share documents and take control of tasks such as accessing a degree audit or registering for classes.

Phone

Online and distance students may not be able to get to campus to meet with an advisor. Other students who have off-campus commitments such as work may also find it difficult to get in to meet with an advisor. Phone appointments may be a viable option if you find yourself in any of these situations. Even though you can't see the advisor, it is still possible to develop a strong relationship with him or her via phone appointments. I recommend preparing for a phone appointment the same way you would for a face-to-face appointment. Prepare your questions ahead of time, and review your degree audit. Be in front of a computer in case you need to navigate to resources, and have something to take notes with. Your advisor may give you URLs, names, or phone numbers that you need, so be prepared to note them. Please do not schedule a phone appointment if you are not prepared or able to devote your time and attention to the advising session. I am frustrated when students schedule appointments for times when they're driving somewhere. They cannot see what I'm trying to show them and cannot write down anything that I have said. The likelihood that you'll remember anything your advisor has said while you are driving is slim. It ends up being a waste of your and the advisor's time.

Walk-In Advising

Walk-in advising refers to a first-come, first-served system of advising. Usually, students literally walk in to the advising center for assistance, but walk-in advising may include impromptu phone calls, as well. Some institutions rely solely on walk-in advising, while others provide it along with an appointment system. In general, walk-in advising is provided for relatively brief exchanges, routine issues, and questions that don't require a great deal of research or follow-up. Walk-in advising sessions tend to be brief, ranging from five to twenty minutes. If your institution provides both appointments and walk-ins, choose walk-in advising when you do not require dedicated time and time-intensive planning. While walk-in advising is convenient because you can drop in when you want, it may result in long wait times. During peak advising periods such as the start of the term, the beginning of registration, and the end of the term, wait times usually increase significantly. Depending on the institution's size and enrollment, wait times have been known to exceed three hours. You can minimize these wait times by seeking advising prior to peak advising periods and by making an appointment.

Group Advising

Some institutions provide advising on a group basis for specific student populations or topics. For example, there might be a group advising session during orientation that is targeted at new students. Academic departments may hold group advising for students in a specific major. Students who are on academic probation or in a specialized program, such as the honors program, may also receive group advising. Many times, group advising sessions are mandatory, and a consequence such as a registration hold will be instituted for nonattendance. Whether mandatory or not, if you have an opportunity to attend a group advising session, do so. The advising staff has determined that the information is important enough to widely disseminate to groups of students and, as such, it is important for you to learn and understand.

Email Advising

I have found that students enjoy the flexibility of emailing their advising questions to an advisor to obtain assistance. The asynchronous nature of email allows you to write down your questions as they occur to you, even if it's at ten o'clock at night. You can send off your questions and move on to the next task at hand. Similarly, advisors can answer the email between student appointments or before and after traditional work hours, should they be inclined to do so. Another benefit of email advising is that your questions, along with the answers, are written down and can be accessed for future reference. On the downside, there is no predicting when you might receive a response to your inquiry. Generally, advisors strive to respond within forty-eight hours, but response time is impacted by the time of year and amount of student traffic. If you have a time-sensitive issue, you may wish to schedule an appointment with an advisor so that you can get the help you need when you need it. Email advising is not appropriate for in-depth discussion about career goals or academic planning. Rather, email advising is meant for addressing specific questions regarding policies, procedures, curricular requirements, and resources.

Roles and Responsibilities in Academic Advising

To get the most out of your advising experience, you should establish a partnership with your advisor. In this partnership, each person will have a role with specific responsibilities. It is important to understand that you are ultimately responsible for the decisions you make and the actions you take. While an advisor can help guide you and provide you information and tools, he or she cannot be held responsible for your success or lack thereof.

Student Role and Responsibilities

Prior to your advising session, do the following:

1. Prepare questions to be discussed.
2. Review your degree audit, and note any areas that are unclear.
3. Consider options you may wish to explore.
4. Review your transcript and degree audit for accuracy (major, program, GPA, etc.).
5. Read the catalog and handbook for policies related to your concerns.
6. Plan to arrive on time. If you're unable to keep your appointment, cancel it prior to the appointment time.

During the advising session, do the following:

1. Use a laptop, a tablet, or paper to write down information such as answers, resources, and contacts.

2. Update your advisor about any decisions, actions, successes, and obstacles you've faced since the last time you spoke.
3. Ask questions that are specific to your immediate needs.
4. Ask about the longer-term implication of decisions.
5. Discuss helpful resources and strategies for success.

Advisor Role and Responsibilities

Advising is a very complex job, and advisors may approach it in different ways. The following list can give you a good idea about what you should expect from your advisor. If none of these occur in the advising session, it is okay to ask for more. For example, if the advisor does not offer information on things you haven't asked about in the session, you can ask, "Are there other things I need to know when considering withdrawing from this class? How will this withdrawal affect me in the long term?"

- Begin the session on time.
- Review student's record for accuracy.
- Provide resources and information related to student questions.
- Identify need-to-know items not asked by the student.
- Help the student explore options and anticipate outcomes of various decisions.
- Answer questions accurately and thoroughly.
- Help the student engage in academic and career planning.
- Facilitate student decision-making and problem-solving.
- Process administrative tasks accurately and in a timely manner.

Three Dangerous Assumptions

While I'd like to say that all advisors, including myself, are perfect and will address your every need, unfortunately, that's not the case. Here are three assumptions that you should be careful to avoid:

1. *Your advisor knows everything.* He or she doesn't. Ask questions and develop a plan of shared responsibility for finding answers.

2. *Your advisor will tell you everything you need to know.* He or she most likely will not. Advisors are busy and tasked with helping large numbers of students, and advisors cannot always anticipate all of your needs and concerns. Take responsibility for researching and asking questions.

3. *Your advisor is infallible.* Your advisor is human and, therefore, fallible. Advisors make mistakes. Take responsibility for reading and understanding policies, procedures, and curricular requirements. Use your tools. Follow up with your advisor if you have been waiting for an answer or action.

Tips for a Successful Advising Experience

1. **Develop a productive advising relationship**. Keep in touch with your advisor regularly. Prepare your thoughts and take responsibility for your decisions and actions.

2. **If you do not believe your advisor is meeting your needs, discuss your concerns with him or her**. Often, frustration comes from a gap between student and advisor expectations.

3. **If you do not feel that you can maintain a productive advising relationship with your assigned advisor, ask the advising administrator if you have the option to be reassigned**. As human beings, we naturally connect with some people rather than others. For instance, I like to talk. I will explain, in detail, what you need to do and explore every avenue with you. If you like a quick, to-the-point discussion, you might not like my style and would be better suited to someone who is more direct. Most likely, if you don't want to work with a certain advisor, the advisor would be glad to support you in your decision to change advisors.

4. **Plan ahead and avoid high-traffic periods.** Find out what times of the year advisors are super busy, and then plan to speak with your advisor before or after that period. Schedule planning meetings prior to the opening of registration. Save questions that are not time sensitive until after the rush. Your advisor will thank you for it.

Questions to Ask Your Advisor

Academic Planning

1. Can you help me understand how to read and understand my degree audit?
2. How can I see my official major or verify that my minor has been added?
3. Can you tell me about this major and what careers or graduate programs it can prepare me for?
4. What's the best way for me to decide how many credits to take each semester?
5. Can I get credit for previous experience or knowledge? Can I test out of anything?

Registration, Problem-Solving, and Decision-Making

6. Are there any implications of this decision on my financial or academic standing?
7. What options do I have pertaining to this issue?
8. What else should I know about this issue or decision?
9. What would help me avoid this problem in the future?
10. Do you have recommendations on what courses I should take and when?
11. How can I find out about registration procedures and deadlines?

Responsibilities and Follow-Up

12. What do I need to do next?
13. What are the next steps that you will be taking?
14. Who is involved in making this decision? When can I expect a decision?
15. What is the process for making this change?
16. How long does it take to process this change?
17. When should I follow up with you if I haven't heard anything?

Resources and Referrals

18. Can you help me locate the catalog? Student handbook? Academic calendar? Schedule of classes?
19. Where can I find additional information about this issue? What resources can I access?
20. Who can help me determine whether this major is the best one for me?
21. How can I find out about career options?

3-2 Your Professors Are Not the Enemy

Your professors are going to be a critical part of your academic success. At times, it will feel like they hold your whole future in their hands, which can make for an intimidating relationship. That's why it's important to understand the real role of faculty and learn how to benefit from their knowledge and skill.

Your professors may be in the field of education for several reasons. They may have entered the field due to a passion for teaching, a passion for their subject matter, or both. As I discussed in chapter 1, your professors are often balancing multiple responsibilities in the areas of teaching, research, and service. Those professors who enjoy the teaching aspect usually take great care to deliver instruction in an engaging, meaningful way. They are available before and after class (time permitting) and will welcome students to their offices to discuss any questions or concerns in order to facilitate the students' success. Faculty members who prefer to focus on research may be assigned upper-division courses and are energized by students who demonstrate interest in the academic subject matter. These professors may not be as receptive to discussing logistics such as how many points you need to pass or personal challenges you face but would be open to discussing the course content and helping you to understand it better. While these are rather broad generalizations, I provide them to set the stage for how to work with your professors, maximize the instructor–student relationship, and avoid conflicts.

Faculty Expectations

As with all people, it is important to see your professors as individuals. Each one may have a different approach to teaching, as well as varied expectations. As you begin each course, take time to learn and understand the professor's expectations regarding student performance. Get to know your professor and help him or her get to know you. Effective communication will go a long way in helping you to avoid conflicts or misunderstandings with your professor.

Read and Understand the Syllabus

The course syllabus is a document that outlines the specific "rules of the game" for the class. Within the syllabus you will find the professor's expectations for the following areas:

- course attendance
- class participation
- grading scale
- calendar of due dates, readings, and assignments
- plagiarism
- code of conduct

Course Attendance

New college students often enjoy the freedoms that come with the transition from high school to college, among which is the perceived flexibility of attending classes. Without threats of detention or suspension to worry about, you are responsible for motivating yourself to get to class. Carefully read the syllabus to determine the policies surrounding the need to miss a class and the consequences of doing so. A common practice is to reduce a student's grade for missed classes or lack of participation. If you need to miss a class, notify your professor as soon as you know you'll have to miss, preferably before the start of class. Keep in touch with your professor before and after the absence. Whatever you do, don't ask, "Did I miss anything important?" for this is insulting to a professor.

Class Participation

Each class is carefully developed by your professor with a specific learning objective in mind. Some classes may be straight lecture, but more often classes include student interaction and group work. Professors want you to be involved in your own learning. Review the syllabus for points that may be assigned for class participation. These are some of the easiest points you can earn and some of the most senseless to lose. Participate by asking questions, answering questions, and contributing to small group and class discussions. This is not high school; no one will judge you for what you say.

Grading Scale

The syllabus will outline exactly what grade you need to pass and how many points you need to earn that grade. Keep track of the points you earn and the corresponding percentage to get an idea of your standing in the class. For instance, if you earn fifteen out of twenty possible points on an assignment, you have earned a 75 percent on the assignment (fifteen divided by twenty).

Calendar of Due Dates

The syllabus will include a calendar of due dates for assignments. It may have specific dates but may also have general dates such as "end of week three." If the course has an online component, there may be a course calendar that you can access electronically. Otherwise, it's up to you to keep track of the dates on your own calendar. Make sure to understand your professor's policy on late work. Is it accepted? If so, for how long? Is there a grade penalty for late work? Don't treat these deadlines as flexible. They are not. If you have difficulty submitting an assignment on time, speak with the professor to discuss your challenges, options, and implications of submitting late work.

Plagiarism

Most syllabi include information about student conduct and plagiarism. Carefully read and understand what plagiarism is and how it can affect you. I have found that most students do not intentionally plagiarize (that is, represent the words of others as their own). Most students just don't know how to cite others' work properly or find the copy and paste functions just a little too convenient. A good rule of thumb is to avoid copying and pasting content from somewhere else into your paper. If you do, put quotation marks around it and tell the reader the source of the quote. I have known several good, sincere students who failed courses because of unintentional plagiarism. It is easy to avoid.

Code of Conduct

Look for information about the student code of conduct in the syllabus. Most likely, the code will refer to plagiarism and cheating. *Code of conduct* also refers to student behavior. Make sure to treat your peers and professors with respect and courtesy. Bullying and taunting should be (thankfully) left back in high school. Students who violate the student code of conduct can be put on probation, suspension, or dismissed from the institution.

Developing Realistic Expectations about Courses

College is not easy. You will experience a shift in academic rigor from high school to college that will most likely increase as you take higher-level courses. As you seek to establish realistic academic expectations, it's important to understand a few basic assertions:

- high grades ≠ approval
- comments ≠ disapproval

Your professors are in the business of helping you learn. Part of that process is to provide you feedback on your papers and tests. Feedback, whether positive or negative, is not a reflection of the professor's feelings about you. The professor may see you as a strong student who will benefit from being pushed to excellence. The professor may notice that you missed the mark on an assignment and want to give you the tools to improve on future assignments. Whatever the feedback, focus on what the professor is telling you and not on what you think it means about his or her feelings about you.

Take Feedback as a Learning Opportunity Rather Than Criticism

Professors are dedicated to helping you learn and develop as a student. It is their primary responsibility and one that most take very seriously. One of the key strategies to facilitate your learning is to provide you feedback, which you may receive in the form of a test score, notes on a paper, or comments about a class presentation. Sometimes, the feedback feels like criticism—"This is what you did wrong!" By providing you feedback, your professor is hoping to provide you the tools and knowledge to be successful in class and in your college program. Take the feedback in this spirit. If the professor gives you additional resources, take advantage of them.

I once had a student who was top in her class and a strong writer who knew the course material. On one of her papers, I made a note to the effect of "Good job! This is a well-written, insightful paper. For future assignments, please make sure to include research which supports your conclusions. This is especially important if you are planning to go on to graduate work." She asked if we could speak about this feedback. During that conversation, I asked her if she was going to graduate school. She said, "I was planning to go on, but after your feedback, I am thinking of dropping out of college since I may not be cut out for it." Wow! She and I were so far apart on our perceptions of her performance. I thought she was one of my best students who had the potential to go on to graduate school. My feedback was intended to help her be successful in future studies, but she took it as a sign that she was not good enough. She jumped right over the "Good job!" "well-written," and "insightful" and focused only on what was missing. Once we spoke and I explained my intentions, along with reinforcing the fact that I thought she was a strong student, she was able to reframe my comments and take them as an opportunity for improvement and growth, not as criticism. Always assume a professor has your best interests in mind. Some additional assumptions that I encourage you to start with each semester are listed below. If you receive what you perceive to be negative feedback, remember them.

- Your professor does not hate you.
- Your professor is not out to get you.
- Your professor is not trying to trick you.
- Your professor does not enjoy failing you.
- Your professor wants you to learn.
- Your professor wants you to succeed.

Establishing good relationships with your professors is a great strategy for academic success and professional growth. Learn what they have to offer, both in and out of the classroom, and take advantage of these important resources!

Types of Feedback

On tests, reflection and research papers, and group projects, your professors will provide you written feedback, usually in the form of questions and statements. Anything less than "Great job!" or "This is a wonderful paper!" can feel like a stinging insult. I encourage you to resist that reaction. In virtually all instances, professors are trying to help you improve by providing comments. Below are some examples of feedback questions and statements.

Questions

- "This is a good point. Where could you find more evidence to back up this statement?"
- "How do you know this to be true?"
- "What was your biggest takeaway from the group project?"

Statements

- "You did not address all of the questions in the assignment."
- "Improper citation. Please see APA manual for citing blog content."
- "This is a good start, but, rather than simply listing your top strengths, I would like to learn how your strengths have helped you succeed in school."

Upon reading this type of feedback, it may be easy to become defensive. For instance, your initial response to the question "How do you know this to be true?" might be "Because I was freakin' there!" or "Because everybody knows that!" Similarly, your response to a statement such as "You did not address all of the questions in the assignment" might be "It would be nice if you told me what I missed." Take a minute to analyze the feedback and consider why the professor would provide it to you in that manner. For instance, "How do you know this to be true?" is a question that encourages students to back up their assertions with research or citations. A professor who indicates that you did not address all the questions is intentionally encouraging you to look back at the assignment and determine, on your own, what you've missed. By doing so, you have a chance to learn how to critically assess your own work.

Sue Ohrablo, Ed.D.

Responding to Feedback

Below is an example of a common student reaction to feedback:

Working hard is a great thing, but in and of itself, it does not mean that you've achieved your goals or met expectations. I could work really hard painting a landscape of the Grand Canyon. I could spend money on buying paint, canvas, and brushes, and I could spend hours carefully working to recreate the beautiful scenery. Ultimately (I guarantee you), it will not come out good. It will not look like much of anything, let alone the Grand Canyon. But, perhaps with art lessons and practice, I could improve. But only through taking in and applying the feedback of art instructors regarding color, shading, and nuances will I have a chance to successfully paint a picture of the Grand Canyon. In this instance, the instructor would not be unfair or biased against me by providing me feedback. In fact, it is just the opposite. By giving me the tools I need, the instructor would be facilitating my learning and skill development.

Instead of blaming the professor, take the feedback as an opportunity to learn. You may learn how to write better, think more critically, analyze more effectively, and research more thoroughly. You may learn to how to better study for and take tests, discover how much time you'll need to dedicate to studying, and maybe simply understand how to discuss your concerns with your professor. You can always learn something new, and I encourage you to open yourself to doing so.

Strategies for Success

Knowing what the professor expects will help you develop realistic expectations about yourself and your role in your education. The following strategies can help you succeed:

- Use the syllabus to learn about the professor's expectations.
  - o Locate due dates and understand policies about absences and late assignments.
  - o Access the grading scale.

- Set goals to meet expectations.
  - o Plan to finish assignments one to two days ahead of the due date.
  - o Complete all assignments.
  - o Include all required information in assignments.

- Pinpoint the key issues the professor has identified.
  - o Review each note the professor provides.
  - o Make a point to resolve each question or learn how to access information in the future.

- Address each issue individually.
  - o Don't get lost in red ink.
  - o Take each comment separately and focus on what you can do to improve.

- Develop strategies to communicate with the professor.
  - o Let your professor know that you want to understand feedback and that you want to improve.
  - o Complaints and defensiveness regarding feedback are not productive.

Building a Successful Student-Faculty Partnership

Establish a Relationship with Your Professor

Sue Ohrablo, Ed.D.

Sit Up Front

In high school, it may not have been cool to sit in the front of class. You may be used to sitting in the back to remain unnoticed. Be noticed! By sitting in the front, your professor will get to know your face, and a connection will start to form. During the class session, a few smiles and head nods will engage your professor and will reinforce his or her tendency to involve you in discussion. While that might seem like something you'd want to avoid, it shouldn't be. Sitting up front and engaging the professor gives you tremendous power and influence over the professor's behavior. An effective practice (from my experience as a student and a professor) is to sit up front and nod when you agree with a statement or understand a concept. Smile at the professor's jokes. After a while, the professor will be conditioned to look at you for feedback. When you come across a concept you don't quite understand, a simple frown or questioning look can trigger the professor to reiterate what he or she was saying or provide more clarification. It's a great way to customize the class session to meet your needs, and most likely, the professor will not be consciously aware it is happening.

Stay after Class

A good way to establish a relationship with your professor is to stay for a minute after class and chat with him or her. Some things you can talk about are a concept from the class, a story you want to share, or a simple question you have. Showing appreciation or providing feedback such as "Thanks for clarifying that concept," or "I thought that activity was great!" are also great strategies for connecting with your professor.

Dos and Don'ts for Engaging Your Professor after Class

Be aware of your surroundings. If other students are waiting, another class is coming in, or your professor is hurriedly packing up, it may not be the best time to engage in a lengthy discussion. Be respectful of your professor's time, in addition to that of other students and professors.

Be authentic. If you are giving thanks or expressing interest in part of the course, be genuine. A professor will be able to tell if you are just "kissing up" or are insincere with your comments.

Avoid complex issues. "Can you show me how to submit my assignment online?" or "Can you explain the concept of …?" are not appropriate for the few minutes you have after class. Use office hours for anything that requires focus and time. After class, you might say, "I'd like to talk with you about [blank]. Do you have time during your office hours today to discuss that?"

Don't be a "hanger-on." While professors love to talk with engaged students, their time is limited. They may only have a few minutes to get from class to class, so talking to students immediately following class may be difficult for them. While it's okay to stop by and say hi occasionally, I don't recommend doing it routinely. If the professor knows that you are going to stop and talk after each class session, he or she may start to avoid you or be distracted when talking with you. Be careful not to overstay your welcome.

Use Office Hours

Office hours are set times that the professor is available to meet with students. Usually, office hours occur several days a week for an hour- or two-hour block of time. Most professors will also make appointments with students who cannot meet during office hours, upon request. It is disheartening and frustrating for professors when their students do not take advantage of office hours, for this is your opportunity to ask questions and obtain further information.

Make it a point to meet with your professor during office hours at least once a semester. Here are some ways you can use office hours:

- Meet early in the semester as a getting-to-know-you opportunity.
- Meet prior to submitting your first assignment to get clarification and direction.
- Seek assistance with topics that are unclear or get feedback on a graded assignment or test.

By dedicating time to meet with your professor, you can get to know him or her, as well as allow him or her to get to know you. By developing a positive relationship with your professor, you can avoid miscommunications or misunderstandings.

Respect the Course and Your Professor

As I mentioned earlier, your professors are in it for the love of the subject or the love of teaching. They don't ask for much from their students. However, professors expect their students to care about their classes and take an active role in their own learning. They also expect students to respect them and the courses themselves. It is difficult for professors when they see their students chatting away with other students, laughing at private jokes, or staring down at phones or laptop screens during class. These behaviors send a message to the professors that you are not interested in learning. Unfortunately, such a message can negatively impact the professor's developing assessment of you. By respecting your professors and the courses, you can earn their respect in return. Following are some ways that you can demonstrate respect:

- *Keep engaged.* Ask and answer questions. Participate in discussions. Take leadership in projects.
- *Keep focused.* Avoid side conversations. Put away electronics and other sources of distraction.
- *Don't try to be the center of attention.* If someone should be at the center of attention, it is your professor. Keep interruptions, conversations, and distracting behavior to a minimum.
- *Don't disrespect the content.* One of the worst questions you can ask a professor is "Did I miss anything important?" The statement implies that sometimes the professor teaches important material and, other times, she does not. Your professor believes that all course content is important.

- *Don't disrespect the professor.* The professor is in charge and sets the rules. Don't assume they can be changed to meet your needs. A statement such as "I have to leave early because I have a doctor's appointment" communicates disrespect of the professor's time. Try to avoid such scheduling conflicts. Do not compound the problem by asking, "Can you tell me what I will miss?" In effect, you are telling the professor that there is something more important you need to do than be in his class and are asking him to teach the content twice.

Course Information and Expectations

Course prefix, number, and title: _____

Professor name: _____

Office location: _____

Phone: _____

Email: _____

Attendance and Participation Policies

Lateness ☐ will ☐ will not be penalized. If yes, how many lates will result in penalty? _____

What is the penalty? _____

Absences ☐ will ☐ will not be penalized. If yes, how many absences will result in penalty? _____

What is the penalty? _____

Class participation ☐ counts ☐ does not count toward my grade.

If yes, what percentage is or number of points are assigned to class participation? _____

Assignments

Submission of late assignments ☐ is ☐ is not allowed.

Submitting a late assignment will negatively affect the grade. ☐ Yes ☐ No

If yes, what is the penalty? _____

Requirements

☐ Tests: How many? _____

☐ Quizzes: How many? _____

☐ Journal entries/blog: How many? _____

☐ Group projects: How many? _____

☐ Research papers: How many? _____

☐ Reflection papers: How many? _____

☐ Other: _____

3-3 Taking Care of Business

Throughout your college experience, you will be required to fill out many forms, run around to numerous offices (or navigate to them online), meet deadlines, and engage in multiple transactions to conduct the business of being a student. This can be a confusing experience and one that often causes students so much frustration that they consider dropping out.

With proper planning, organization, and communication, you can greatly reduce the amount of frustration you experience as you try to get things done. In fact, you will find that most everyone who works at your institution is willing and happy to help you. By establishing positive relationships with the staff in the admissions, financial aid, registrar's, academic advising, and other student support offices, you can smooth the way to a hassle-free experience.

Get Ahead of the Game

Planning ahead is a good way to avoid long lines and anxious people. If possible, budget at least two weeks before a deadline to conduct your business. This helps you to avoid the rush and also gives you time to make changes or submit additional information if needed.

Organize Your Information

Keeping yourself organized will reduce the chance of becoming confused or frustrated. Keep all of your forms, documents, and correspondence in one place for easy access. Develop a system that works for you, whether it is in paper or electronic version.

- Create separate folders such as "Financial Aid 2018" or "Registration."
- Organize your emails for easy retrieval.

    o   Use the "categorize" feature to color code and sort emails by topic. Major categories should include Financial Aid, Registrar, Bursar, Housing, Academics, and Advising.

    o   Create subfolders in your in-box to save emails by department. Right-click on your in-box, select "New," and title your folder.

- Mark dates and deadlines on your calendar as soon as you become aware of them.
- Develop tasks and to-do items:

Stay Calm

It is important to establish clear, professional communication with faculty, staff, and administrators within your institution, whether it is in person, on the phone, or via email. During peak periods, emotions can run high and tempers short. By keeping a respectful tone, you can achieve your goals and get what you need. Inflammatory, accusatory language and behavior will not help you resolve your problems or obtain answers, so no matter how anxious or angry you may become, avoid saying or doing anything that will make matters worse.

Phrases to Use	Phrases to Avoid
• I appreciate your taking the time to help me. • I know you are busy, but … • I hope you can help me. • Thank you for your assistance. • Have a great day! • You were so helpful last time I spoke with you. • I appreciate you.	• I demand to speak with someone! • I refuse to leave until I get some answers. • You never … • You always … • Why didn't you … • It's not my fault. • You should have … • This is ridiculous! • I pay tuition!

Ask Questions

It is important to speak up and ask questions when you are unsure or need more information. Don't worry about seeming stupid. You are here to learn, and this is all part of the learning process. Before meeting with someone from a department, make sure you develop a list of questions so that you'll remember to ask them. Using the notes feature on your smartphone is a quick and easy way to keep a running list of your questions handy. Use the "Questions to Ask Business Offices" checklist for a guide to the type of questions you might want to ask.

Understand Jargon and Acronyms

We in higher education love our acronyms. Some of us forget that what is common knowledge to us is foreign to you. Ask for clarification. By understanding what the acronyms mean, it is easier to remember their meaning. As you learn what each acronym means, you can begin to speak the language of the institution.

Help Us Help You

In addition to planning, being organized, and communicating effectively, it is important to understand where you fit into the institution at large. You are one of many students. I hate to say it and will avoid saying it to your face at all costs—after all, I want you to feel special and valued because you are. But this is our reality. We potentially work with hundreds of students each day and may not be able to attend to your needs when you first reach out to us. Please be patient. Understand that, while we do our best to help you as quickly and as thoroughly as we can, the sheer volume of students we see may be a factor in the assistance you receive. You can use the following strategies to maximize the effectiveness of service and minimize the response time.

Identify Yourself

By providing as much information up front as you can, you enable staff to research your records and investigate your concerns. The more information that is missing (such as your student ID number or the spelling of your last name), the longer it will take to respond to you.

In person: Be prepared to provide your first and last name, as well as your student ID number. Bring your college ID with you as identification.

Voice mail: Spell your name when you leave a phone message, and include your student ID number. Don't forget to provide your phone number. Briefly describe the problem or question you have, and provide a good time to return the call. Do not rush or mumble.

Email: Include your first and last name, as well as your student ID, in every email you send. Make sure to clearly state your concern or question. Do not assume that the reader has previous knowledge of your issue or is in possession of prior correspondence.

I love my students and the relationships we've developed. I try very hard to get to know them as people. But even through all these efforts, when a student calls and says, "Hi, it's Melanie!" or "I'm following up on that class we discussed," chances are good that I will not know which Melanie is calling or which class we discussed. Even though you may have spoken to me just three hours earlier, I have probably worked with fifteen or more students since then. By providing comprehensive information, you can maximize the assistance you receive and minimize the number of questions the staff member has to ask you in order to help. For example, I would prefer to hear, "Hi. It's Melanie Smith. I'm following up with you to find out if you got approval for me to take MAT 123. Remember that it is full and you said you'd reach out to the department chair?"

The truth of the matter is that, in addition to successfully taking courses, you will be required to fill out forms, meet deadlines, and conduct transactions with many departments throughout the institution. Don't let this experience get you down or stress you out. Even though it may feel like we are throwing roadblocks in your way or making you jump through unnecessary hoops, please remember that we are trying to help you the best we can and have your best interests in mind.

Developing Realistic Expectations about Student Services

Okay, here I will lay out what you can expect in the most honest way I can. You can expect to be frustrated. Whether it's financial aid, advising, the registrar, or another student services department, you most likely will encounter a policy, procedure, or situation that frustrates you. At certain times of the year, there are long lines to wait in and delayed responses to emails and phone calls. People will be working hard to keep up with student traffic, but, in doing so, they may come across as curt or uncaring. You will also encounter a great deal of paperwork, as forms (electronic or paper) are needed for just about everything in higher education. You will find policies that you believe are unfair but, nonetheless, still must adhere to.

When you first explored options for college, you may have been proactively contacted by admissions offices from various institutions. You may have received brochures, phone calls, and invitations to events. Your calls may have been quickly returned and requests for appointments promptly addressed. Once you enroll in college, the speed and responsiveness may slow down. I've heard many students state, "Now that they've got my money, no one wants to help me!" The reality is that there is a natural transition from being recruited to being enrolled. Many of the processes that you will go through are complicated and require more time than those during the recruitment phase. A ten-minute admissions meeting is replaced by an hour-long advising session. There are more enrolled students than there are new students, so the available resources are spread across more students.

I am not telling you this to discourage you but rather to help you develop a realistic framework for understanding and avoiding frustration. Use the following strategies to maintain positive interactions with institution personnel.

Prepare a List of Questions Ahead of Time

By preparing a list of questions prior to speaking with student services representatives, you can reduce the number of phone calls and visits to various departments. You can also reduce the amount of time you spend with them, which helps if you're in a rush. Preparing for your meeting helps avoid delays caused by "Oh, yeah, just one more thing …" If you've ever been behind the guy in the grocery store who is checking out and realizes he forgot to get lettuce, you know how annoying this can be as you wait for his kid to run and get it.

Make Appointments

You might think that it is most convenient to drop in to offices or call them when you have free time, whether it's between classes or at the end of the day. The problem is that, if you are between classes, so is everyone else. If departments offer the option for an appointment, take it. An appointment is dedicated time for you to meet with people who can help you with little to no distractions. Appointments help you to avoid long lines or wait times.

Avoid High-Traffic Periods

Find out the peak periods for student traffic. Just ask anyone who works in the department, and they'll be able to tell you. Typically, the following times are very hectic in higher education.

1. Two weeks prior to through the end of the first week of the semester
2. The first two weeks of registration
3. The last two weeks of registration
4. Add/drop week (first week of classes)
5. End of the semester (especially May)

Plan to meet with your advisor, get your financial aid, settle your bill, and take care of any other interactions you need to accomplish outside of the peak periods. You will be able to significantly reduce your frustration by doing so.

Research on Your Own

I always felt bad for students who waited for me to return calls or emails regarding simple things they could have accomplished themselves. During peak periods, they might have waited a week to find out the name of the course they needed when they could have looked it up on their degree audit. When that occurred, I always made sure to provide them the resources they needed so that they could be more self-sufficient in the future and reduce their frustration due to wait times. Even though you may think it's easier just to call an office rather than look it up, you'll find that you'll get what you need quicker if you use available resources instead. Most college websites and intranet portals are easily searchable and provide you the forms and information you will need.

Don't Wait until the Last Minute

Some things take time. Although changing your major may seem easy, it may not be. You may have to fill out a request form and then have it signed by several administrators. Once approved, it may need to be entered into your student record. While your part is reasonably quick, the subsequent steps may not be. You might think that requesting a seat in a closed course requires a simple yes or no, when in fact it is a complicated request that may require you to justify your need, have to be reviewed by faculty and administrators, and need to be processed by administrative personnel. If you really need a course, make sure to register on the first day registration opens. Budget some time for the processing of your requests. I recommend at least a two-week period for any special actions or requests that need to be processed or reviewed.

Ask for Clarification

If you don't understand, ask. If it still doesn't make sense, ask again. We can be confusing as heck when we use all of our acronyms and jargon. We can forget that processes that we deal with all day, every day, are new to you. Don't be embarrassed or shy. Ask for clarification on anything that does not make sense to you. Too often, I had to help students clean up a problem they encountered when they didn't do what was expected of them simply because they didn't really understand what they needed to do.

Ask for Next Steps

When you've completed your conversation or meeting, ask what the next steps will be. What do they need to do? What do you need to do? Is there anything else you should know? Recently, a colleague of mine went to the Department of Motor Vehicles to register a vehicle. He had been told to bring the title. After waiting an hour, he was told he needed the original title, not a copy. So he went home to retrieve the original. After waiting another hour on his second attempt, he was told that he also needed the bill of sale and could not get the registration without it. The need for a third visit could have been avoided if the staff member had said, "Bring the original title and bill of sale when you return." Unfortunately, customers and student services staff don't always think to do that. Therefore, take it upon yourself to ask, "Is there anything else I need to bring when I come back?"

Thank People

Student services personnel (and anyone who works in higher education) are not in it for the money. They work in their jobs because they want to. They are dedicated to helping you achieve your educational goals. By simply and consistently thanking those who help you, you can avoid conflict and reduce frustration. I can't tell you how much it meant to me when, as I was frantically trying to return student calls and reply to emails, a student would say, "I know how crazy busy you must be right now, and I appreciate the time you are taking with me." If you are able to establish friendly relationships with personnel across campus, you will improve the quality of service you experience.

Questions to Ask Business Offices

General Questions

1. When will I have to [submit this form, make a request, make a decision, etc.] by?
2. Is there anything else you need from me?
3. What are the next steps?
4. When can I expect to [hear a decision, see a change, get an answer, etc.]?
5. Do I need a paper form, or can I submit it online?
6. What does [an initialism—e.g., FAFSA, SAP, CRN] stand for?

Bursar's Office

1. When is my payment due?
2. What are the penalties for late payment?
3. Will I be dropped from my courses if I don't pay by the deadline?
4. Do you have a payment plan? If so, what are the details?
5. If I go into collections, will it go on my credit report?
6. What is the difference between internal and external collections?

Financial Aid

1. What academic requirement do I need to meet in order to receive financial aid?
2. How early can I apply for financial aid, and what is the deadline?
3. How do I determine if I am an independent or dependent student?
4. What is the deadline for applying for financial aid for next year?
5. What documentation will I need to provide when I apply for financial aid?
6. How do I get my financial aid applied to my bill? Is there anything I need to do to make sure the bill is paid?
7. What is the difference between financial aid being awarded versus disbursed?
8. What is a financial aid award, and why do I have to accept it?
9. When can I expect my financial aid to be disbursed to me?
10. What happens if I am awarded more financial aid than the cost of the bill? How will I receive that money?
11. How do I use financial aid to buy books?
12. Can I use financial aid to pay a past balance on my account?
13. What is Satisfactory Academic Progress (SAP), and how does it affect my eligibility to receive financial aid?
14. I need money to live before my financial aid is disbursed. Do you have an emergency loan fund?

Registrar

1. When does registration begin?
2. What is a late registration period, and what are the penalties for registering during it?
3. What is the difference between a drop and withdrawal?
4. Can I drop/add without financial or academic penalty? When is the drop/add period?
5. Do I have to pay for copies of my transcript? Can I access an unofficial transcript on my own?
6. I need proof of enrollment. How to I obtain that?
7. When is commencement? How do I participate?

Disabilities Services

1. How do I get accommodations for a disability in college?
2. What documentation do I need to provide?
3. What are the differences between disability services in high school versus college?
4. How will faculty know that I receive accommodations?
5. To whom do I speak about housing accommodations?

CHAPTER 4

OVERCOMING OBSTACLES AND RESOLVING CONFLICT

4-1 Understanding Your New Role as a College Student

The transition from high school to college is not always an easy one. For years, your family and teachers have set parameters within which you have had to operate. You came to learn what to expect and what was expected of you through years of reinforcement.

When you enter college, no one is there to open the door and lay out expectations for you. No one will tell you what to expect, either. During orientation and the first week of classes, the institution's faculty and staff will outline basic policies, procedures, and protocols. Courses such as freshman seminar will help you develop a set of expectations for college as well as help you to understand what is expected of you.

Transition to College

Let's look at where you've been and what you'll be facing in college.

Structure

High School

Your first twelve or thirteen years of education have been highly structured. For the most part, all your classes have been identified and scheduled for you. You may have had some say about electives or academic tracks, but for the most part, those decisions were made for you. You also had a set schedule that dictated where you had to be and when. It was obvious when you weren't where you were supposed to be, and specific consequences were attached to noncompliance. Your entire day was structured by the school, and you were committed to attending from morning until afternoon.

College

Now that you're going to college, you are responsible for structuring your own day. You will decide if you take only afternoon classes so that you can sleep until noon, and you will decide if you avoid Friday classes entirely. You will even decide whether you want to go to class at all. While this all sounds great, it can be a big challenge to suddenly take responsibility for your own schedule and establish structure. In reality, you can't have it just the way you want it. If the math class you need is offered only on Monday, Wednesday, and Friday, then you need to take it even if you don't want to.

You'll also need to fill in the free time on your own. When you first see a college schedule, you may be excited to see how much free time you have. It will look a lot different from your high school schedule. So is college easier? No. It's just that the responsibility for filling in the blanks is now yours, not the institution's. Let's look at how your first semester might look to you.

	Monday	Tuesday	Wednesday	Thursday	Friday
8:00 a.m.	*Woo-hoo! Sleep late!*				
9:00 a.m.	MAT 101	ENG 110	MAT 101	ENG 110	MAT 101
10:00 a.m.	ORI 100		ORI 100		ORI 100
11:00 a.m.	*Hang out with friends in student union*				
12:00 p.m.	HIS 101	BIO 110	HIS 101	BIO 110	HIS 101
1:00 p.m.	*I can't believe I'm done for the day! I'm freeeee!*				
2:00 p.m.					

While all of that free time looks great, it is not really free. You'll have to budget your own study time, work schedule (if you plan to work), social time, and time for rest. By structuring the time that you are not in class, you will develop a schedule that will meet your needs. If you use the unstructured approach, as in the above example, you may find yourself cramming for exams late into the night or may find that you missed the opportunity to ask your professor a question you had because you missed her office hours.

When you develop a schedule, ask yourself the following:

1. Am I a morning or afternoon person? Schedule your harder classes during your peak performance period if possible.
2. What courses am I not looking forward to? What time should I schedule them to maximize my chances of staying awake? What classes do I like that I can schedule nearby so I have something to look forward to?
3. Do I want to or have to work? If so, how many hours per week?
4. Are there clubs and activities that I want to join? When do they meet?

With these things in mind, your realistic schedule begins to take shape.

	Monday	Tuesday	Wednesday	Thursday	Friday
8:00 a.m.	*Breakfast in dining hall. Budget fifteen minutes to and from.*				
9:00 a.m.	MAT 101	ENG 110	MAT 101	ENG 110	MAT 101
10:00 a.m.	ORI 100		ORI 100		ORI 100
11:00 a.m.	*Ask professor follow-up questions. Travel to class. Rest.*				
12:00 p.m.	HIS 101	BIO 110	HIS 101	BIO 110	HIS 101
1:00 p.m.					
2:00 p.m.	*On-campus job*	*Study for math and history*	*On-campus job*	*Study for math and history*	*On-campus job*
3:00 p.m.					

Policies and Procedures

High School

Probably as far back as you can remember in school, you've been told where to go, what to do, and how to do it. If you attended the same high school for four years, you probably got tired of hearing the same policies explained year after year. You most likely had to have your parent or another family member sign something that assured the school you had read and shared it. You learned to know and understand what was expected of you and how to accomplish what you needed to.

College

As discussed in chapters 1 and 2, you'll be responsible for locating and learning many policies and procedures on your own. We don't hand you a list of rules when you walk in the door. Even if we did, you would most likely not read them. It is important that you know where to find policies and procedures and ask questions about them if you don't understand something. As I've mentioned earlier, the phrases "Nobody told me" and "I didn't know" will not protect you from negative consequences. Although we work hard to inform you and provide you many resources, ultimately you are responsible for your own decisions and actions. This can be a tough transition, as it is very different from high school.

Peer Network

High School

Many students go through their entire elementary, middle school, and high school years with the same kids, growing up together along the way. Others move around a bit and change schools but still have a chance to develop friendships. While your group of friends may have changed over the years, you are most likely familiar with many students. You see the same faces in class year after year, and you develop some close, trusting relationships with friends.

College

No matter whether you go away to college or stay local, you will most likely not know as many people as you did in high school. Even if your friends do attend the same college as you, they may be taking different courses at different times at different locations on campus. It is inevitable that you will need to develop a new peer network. The good news is that all the cliques, reputations, gossip, and bullying are gone. You can start anew and develop friendships with the people you want to, not just the people who live down the street. If it's hard for you to meet new people, start small. Getting to class a few minutes early can allow you to talk to the person who's sitting next to you and get to know him or her a bit better. When working in pairs or doing group work, pick new people to work with so you can get to know more people. When I was teaching a freshman seminar course, I was amazed—and pleased—to see close friendships develop over the course of just one semester. If a student was running late, typically one of his friends would hold up a phone and say, "He just texted me. He got a flat tire, but he's at the light coming on to campus." It's important to develop a peer network when you get to college. It is not always easy, but even getting to know one to three people on whom you can rely and hang out with will make you feel more connected and comfortable.

Locus of Control

High School

Just as I mentioned in my discussion about structure, there will be a significant difference in the locus of control between high school and college. What do I mean by *locus of control*? It's the way you see the world and how much control you perceive you have. Since, in high school, you didn't have a whole lot of individual control or say in decision-making, you may have come to develop an external locus of control. That is, your life has been primarily controlled by outside forces, and those forces will cause things to happen to you.

College

In college, we wave a magic wand and expect you to have an internal locus of control, which means that the events that happen in your life are determined by your own beliefs and actions. As you adopt an internal locus of control, you begin to understand that you can directly contribute to the outcomes that result from your decisions and behaviors. When you enter college, we tell you to "take responsibility," even though you may not have had to do so before. While moving from an external to an internal locus can be scary, it is also incredibly freeing and empowering.

You Are Not a Customer

Contrary to popular belief, you are not a customer in college. You are a student. Customers spend their money in exchange for a product or service, but students invest their money to enter a mutually agreed upon educational relationship. Unlike customers, students are expected to perform to a certain standard and adhere to specific protocols. When you buy a TV as a customer, there is no expectation as to what shows you will watch. When you take your clothes to the dry cleaners, there is no expectation as to the style of clothes they will or will not clean. Being a student is similar to the relationship you have with your doctor. Just as you cannot expect your doctor to cure you if you don't take the prescribed medicines and follow directions for bed rest, you cannot expect your professor to teach you simply by paying your tuition.

Recently, one of my students referred to me in an email as a "service provider." In all honesty, I about went through the roof. I have spent my entire career working to support and educate college students, partnering with them to help them achieve success. This statement was disrespectful and demeaning, and it devalued the relationship between student and professor. While I am not the type of professor who would let my feelings affect how I work with students, there are professors who might. We are only human.

I strongly encourage you to avoid any statement that indicates that you should be treated a certain way or have your expectations met because you are a customer. "I pay a lot of tuition so ..." and "I pay your salary ..." are two phrases to avoid at all costs. You will not achieve any positive outcomes by uttering these phrases but could negatively impact your relationships with institutional personnel and faculty.

Please keep in mind the following thoughts, especially when you begin to experience frustration. They may sound harsh, but they are true whether you like it or not.

- Things are more complex than they seem.
- You can't get what you want at the exact minute you want it.
- People are human—and fallible.
- You are not the only student who needs help.

4-2 Identifying Your Options

A great way to overcome obstacles is to avoid them entirely. Obstacles occur when you have set a plan in motion but something gets in the way of your achieving your objectives. For instance, you may plan to take BIO 101, MAT 111, PSY 102, and ENG 200 in the upcoming semester. However, when you go to register, you find out that all the sections of PSY 102 are full, and your favorite English teacher is not teaching ENG 200. This might feel like an obstacle because you are not getting what you had planned. By having a plan B and a plan C, you are less likely to become frustrated and still achieve your goals.

You always have options. I encourage you to keep that in mind throughout your college career. This is especially helpful if someone tells you no. If you encounter a no, ask about options. While some faculty and staff are adept at outlining your options to you, others may not be. If you can learn to identify your options on your own, you will feel more in control and be less likely to be thrown off course when something does not go the way you had planned.

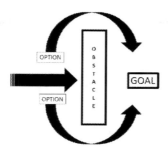

To identify options, you will first need to identify the variables involved in what you are trying to achieve. For instance, when planning your course schedule, consider the following:

- time of day
- course subjects
- professors
- sequences
- semester or term
- credit load

Then, determine the must-haves and work down from there. If you must finish all of your classes by 3:00 p.m. so that you can attend your sports team practice and the only open sections of BIO 101 are after 3:00 p.m., you'll need to make a decision.

- Is there another science course that I could take that would meet at the time I need?
- Is BIO 101 offered every semester? If so, can I take it in a later semester and take something else in its place?
- Is there an open evening section that won't conflict with my practices or games?
- Can I request that a seat be opened for me in one of the full sections?

After the must-haves, consider your priorities and limitations:

- Although I want to take Dr. Smith, I would rather not wait until he teaches this course again.

- I wanted to take fifteen credits this semester.
- I need to take PSY 102 this semester because it is a prerequisite to my major courses.
- Although I prefer BIO 101, I can take any lab science.
- I need to take MAT 111 because it is offered only once a year.

As you evaluate your options, consider the following:

- What is the most important part of plan A that I want to keep?
- If I don't take it this semester, what will happen?
- How will this new plan impact me in the future?
- What are the advantages of plan A? Plan B? Plan C?

You can use this process of identifying options for issues you face outside of the classroom, as well. For instance, perhaps you learn that to remain in good standing with financial aid, you must successfully earn fifteen credits and raise your GPA to a 3.0 by the end of the academic year. If you run into a closed course, you can take another in its place or make alternative arrangements to take the course you want and meet the financial aid requirements.

Plan A	Plan B	Plan C	
Fall Semester:	Fall Semester:	Fall Semester:	Summer Semester:
ENG 200	ENG 200	ENG 200	BIO 101
PSY 102	PSY 102	PSY 102	
BIO 101	CHM 101	MAT 111	
MAT 111	MAT 111	HIS 300	
HIS 300	SOC 202		

Do you prefer plan B, which helps you to avoid taking summer classes? Or do you like the idea of taking biology, which is a difficult subject for you, by itself in the summer, allowing you to better focus on it? Is the likelihood of your getting the grades you need to be in good standing better if you just take twelve credits in the fall?

As you encounter obstacles, map out alternative options to get where you want to go. Think of it as driving to a location only to find an accident or road closure blocking your route. Your GPS will automatically reroute you based on its available knowledge of alternative routes that will lead you to your destination. Develop your own, internal GPS that allows you to reroute and help you get where you are going.

4-3 Building Your Resilience

I spend a lot of time training advisors and faculty members on helping students build resilience—that is, how to help students overcome obstacles and successfully complete their studies. But this is not something anyone else can ultimately do for you. Your attitudes, beliefs, and behaviors are going to determine the likelihood of remaining enrolled in college. By objectively looking at your perception of the world and how it impacts you, you can build your resilience to get through the tough times.

Up until now, your support system may have consisted of friends from school, your family, and teachers you know and trust. If you've gone away to college, your support system may be smaller and less trusted. Before, if you had a conflict with a teacher or friend, you probably had at least one person with whom you could exchange ideas or vent. If you've gone away to college and don't know anyone to help give you perspective ("Oh, you know her, she's always like that. She's harmless."), it may be harder to manage the stress and negative feelings that you are experiencing.

Inevitably, you will encounter challenges that threaten to derail you. You may have a roommate who makes you decide you'd rather go home and attend a local college rather than put up with her. You might encounter a professor who is unreasonably demanding and decide to change your major as a result. The process for obtaining financial aid may be so complicated that you give up and decide to forget about college. While these examples are extreme, unfortunately, I see these types of things happen every semester. It breaks my heart when students leave the institution for reasons that are, in my opinion, fixable.

Resilience is a characteristic that allows you to successfully adapt to challenges that you encounter. It's your ability to get through tough times by reevaluating your expectations and options. It's removing potential threats to your well-being through reframing how you perceive and react to difficulties. The more resilient you are, the more likely you are to stay on course.

Managing Negative Experiences

A popular approach to examining and addressing negative thinking is called Rational Emotive Behavior Therapy (REBT) (Ellis 2001, Bishop 2004). Without getting too clinical, I'll lay out the basic takeaways that can help you better manage your reactions to adverse situations.

- *R = Rational*: What you think about what has happened; the conclusions that you draw
- *E = Emotive*: How you feel when something happens; your thoughts directly contribute to your feelings about an event
- *B = Behavior*: The actions you take as a result of an event; your behavior results from a combination of your thoughts and feelings

In REBT, you are encouraged to examine the impact that events have on you and to follow your line of thinking to identify subsequent feelings and behaviors. By understanding your reactions to a specific event, you can begin to challenge your thinking, especially if it is negative, and change your emotional and behavioral responses.

Let's break it down and look at examples:

A = activating event. Something happens that upsets you. These are some examples of an activating event:

- getting a failing grade on a test
- your roommate's playing loud music
- your academic advisor's not completing the form you asked him to

B = beliefs. Beliefs can be rational (in other words, logical and might be true) or irrational (usually exaggerated conclusions you draw without proof). Examples include the following:

- I failed this test. I will fail the course. I am not cut out for college. I should just quit.
- My roommate doesn't care about me. I hate my roommate. I don't fit in.
- The advising office always gets things wrong. My advisor does not care about students. He is incompetent. I give up.

C = consequences. This is your reaction to the event and your beliefs about it. Some examples are as follows:

- Develop anxiety about passing the next test and the course. Develop anger toward the professor, whom you believe to be unfair. Consider withdrawing from the course or changing your major.
- Develop depression and feelings of isolation because of your conflict with your roommate. Stop talking to your roommate. Consider asking for new room assignment.
- Get angry with your academic advisor. Refuse to submit another form. Demand to speak to the supervisor. Consider switching colleges.

Let's take one of those examples and put A, B, and C together in a line so you can see what happens in real time:

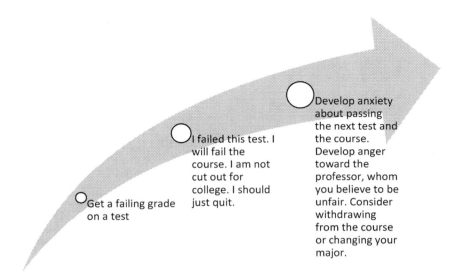

Get a failing grade on a test

I failed this test. I will fail the course. I am not cut out for college. I should just quit.

Develop anxiety about passing the next test and the course. Develop anger toward the professor, whom you believe to be unfair. Consider withdrawing from the course or changing your major.

Sound familiar? It should. We engage in this type of thinking and reacting all the time, usually with no awareness of the process happening at all. Road rage? Yup. Let's take a look:

> A car cuts you off in traffic. → That guy doesn't care about anyone but himself. He should not be allowed to drive. He needs to learn that he's not the only car on the road! → This hand gesture will show him that he can't get away with it! I'll drive up on his bumper to show him that I can be just as reckless.

So now what? The first step is to become aware of what happened, what beliefs and reactions you had to it, and what your response will be. Now, in order to change negative into positive, we need to introduce two new elements.

D = disputing. Challenge the truth of your beliefs. Identify irrational thinking. These are some examples of disputing:

- Where is the evidence that failing the test will make me fail the course?
- Is it true that, just because my roommate plays loud music, she does not like me?
- Is it really that awful that the form was not completed when I expected it to be? It's annoying but not the end of the world.

E = *effective thoughts*. Substitute negative, self-destructive thoughts and emotions with thoughts that will more effectively help you get through. This step is a way to turn around your thinking.

- I will use this experience as motivation to study more effectively. I will meet with the professor about missed material.
- I am learning to live with diverse people. Tomorrow (after a good night's sleep), I will speak with my roommate about my concerns.
- I guess my advisor is very busy at this time of year. Next time, I'll make sure to meet with my advisor earlier and see if I can accomplish the same thing online.

I have found common triggers among students who are upset, angry, and anxious. Below is a partial list of triggers and ways to dispute negative thinking.

Not getting your way	Should I expect that I always get things done my way?
Financial loss	Is it true that, if I fail this class, I will lose money? Have I really wasted my money just because I failed this test?
Immediate needs not fulfilled	Is it realistic that my needs should be fulfilled immediately when I need something? Are there factors that would prevent someone from helping me right when I request help?
Lack of academic progress	Does failing this test result in a failing course grade? If I go on probation, will I be kicked out of the program?
Perceived bias or discrimination	Is it likely that this person is biased against me? Could there be other reasons for this behavior? How are other students treated?
Perceived lack of assistance	Is it reasonable to believe that I might need to wait due to high student traffic? Is it possible that my expectations regarding service are unrealistic? Is there something I can do to avoid this in the future?
Lack of information	Are there other sources that can provide me the information I need? What resources should I rely on?
Lack of direction	Do I have time before choosing a major? Does being undecided mean that I will never find a career I enjoy?
Fear of the unknown	Just because I don't know what's ahead, is that reason to fear it? Have I successfully accomplished other things even though I didn't understand everything right away?

I will admit that this process is not easy. We are used to immediately drawing conclusions and reacting to situations without even being aware we are doing it. It will take time to internalize this approach in order to build up your resilience to negative events. However, once you learn to see things from a different perspective, you will be able to overcome obstacles and persist in your personal and academic life.

Keeping Self-Talk in Check

Use the guide below to analyze an event that upsets, angers, or frustrates you. Identify what you are telling yourself and the options for alternative thinking.

Event (what happened?):

Thoughts that immediately come to mind as a result of the event:

Are the thoughts (beliefs, assumptions, conclusions):

☐   True?

☐   Negative?

☐   Distracting?

Feelings about the event:

Alternative ways of thinking about the event:

How can I react in a more positive, growth-oriented way?

CHAPTER 5

Looking Ahead

I've written this book hoping to make the transition to college a little easier for you and your family. Knowing where to go, whom to talk to, and what to ask can go a long way as you're trying to navigate a new environment. I don't expect that, once you've read this book, you'll be an expert at navigating college and will avoid obstacles and problems. However, hopefully you'll have the tools and skills you need to minimize their impact.

I encourage you to do the work within this book; fill out the checklists and complete the tools provided. Keep these resources close by in case you need them. Develop systems that work for you and use them.

Long-Term Planning

Just as you have done with this book, I recommend that you continue to plan and thoughtfully engage in decision-making. Each year, you will have new adventures and challenges. Look ahead to avoid missing out on opportunities and deadlines. Below is a partial list of steps you should take each year as you move through your degree.

Freshman Year

- Figure out how many credits you can successfully take each semester.
- Develop friendships.

- Learn your way around campus, and identify important offices.
- Learn about your major requirements, and begin academic planning.
- Take a freshman seminar course.
- Take a career exploration course.

Sophomore Year

- Research career opportunities for your major, and confirm or change your major, as appropriate.
- Establish positive relationships with at least two professors.
- Consider adding a minor.
- Investigate internship opportunities.
- Meet with an advisor to make sure you are taking the right courses.

Junior Year

- Visit the career services office to explore career options and develop a résumé.
- Consider graduate school options and research graduate schools.
- Research graduate and professional school admissions tests (e.g., GRE, GMAT ®, LSAT ®).
- Participate in an internship program.
- Delve into your major courses.

Senior Year

- Apply to graduate school.
- Finalize résumé.
- Participate in an internship program.
- Seek letters of reference.
- Meet with an advisor to verify that you are on track to graduate.
- Participate in activities and events that will broaden your professional knowledge and contacts.
- Begin your job search.

Tracking Milestones

Take time to enjoy your college experience. In addition to the stressors, ups and downs, and uncertainties, you will meet some amazing people, form close relationships, learn new things, and mature in all aspects of your life. Keep track of the little things that you accomplish and give yourself credit for those accomplishments. Below is a list of milestones that you may achieve throughout your college career. Check off each one as it occurs and feel free to add to the list if you want!

Final Thoughts

I wish you and your family all the best as you begin your higher education journey! Enjoy each day and consider any challenges you face as learning opportunities. Take time to relax and have fun, but don't lose sight of your long-term goal of degree completion. Use the plentiful resources that are available to you and partner with your institution to have a rich, successful college experience.

Milestone Checklist

- ☐ Attended orientation
- ☐ Met my first friend
- ☐ Passed my first test
- ☐ Connected with a professor I like
- ☐ Attended a sporting event
- ☐ Attended a party
- ☐ Met someone I'd like to date
- ☐ Registered for my second semester
- ☐ Learned something new about my major or intended career
- ☐ Successfully dealt with a stressful situation
- ☐ Reviewed my degree audit
- ☐ Met with an academic advisor
- ☐ Had lunch or dinner with someone new
- ☐ Did something to improve my health
- ☐ Joined a club
- ☐ Had a positive group-project experience
- ☐ Sought help from a tutoring or writing center
- ☐ Learned how to use a new technology
- ☐ Contributed to class discussion
- ☐ Bought my first T-shirt or sweatshirt with the school's logo
- ☐ Wrote a paper that I'm proud of
- ☐ Learned how to get around campus without a map
- ☐ Asked another student for help
- ☐ Slept an average of seven to eight hours for five days in a row
- ☐ Attended a student success workshop (managing stress, study tips, test-taking, etc.)
- ☐ Asked a professor for help
- ☐ Took on a leadership role
- ☐ Rode on public transportation
- ☐ Called my family for support
- ☐ Read the catalog
- ☐ Located campus safety emergency call lights or phones
- ☐ Arranged for an escort to walk me to class or my car
- ☐ Planned next year's living arrangements
- ☐ Learned all my professors' names
- ☐ Sought out career counseling
- ☐ Completed my first set of classes
- ☞ Earned my first A
- ☐ Earned my highest grade so far

WORKS CITED

Bishop, F. M. 2004. *Rational Emotive Behavior Therapy: The Basics*. Presented at the SMART Recovery National Training Conference, Phoenix, AZ. Retrieved from http://www.smartrecovery.org/resources/library/For Family Volunteers Professionals/basics-of-rebt.pdf.

Ellis, E. 2001. *Overcoming Destructive Beliefs, Feelings, and Behaviors: New Directions for Rational Emotive Behavior Therapy*. Amherst, NY: Prometheus Books.

For more information contact the author at
www.sueohrablo.com or sohrablo@outlook.com

To obtain full-sized copies of the forms and checklists
within this book, visit www.sueohrablo.com

Get Off That Pew and Find Something to Do!

A Guide for Activating Kingdom-Building Ministries

Helen B. Britt

Spreading the Gospel through innovative ways as the church continues to grow and thrive during the 21st century by bringing faith, hope, spiritual gifts and God's Word in total harmony.

WESTBOW
P R E S S®
A DIVISION OF THOMAS NELSON
& ZONDERVAN

WestBow Press books may be ordered through booksellers or by contacting:

WestBow Press
A Division of Thomas Nelson & Zondervan
1663 Liberty Drive
Bloomington, IN 47403
www.westbowpress.com
1 (866) 928-1240

Because of the dynamic nature of the Internet, any web addresses or links contained in this book may have changed since publication and may no longer be valid. The views expressed in this work are solely those of the author and do not necessarily reflect the views of the publisher, and the publisher hereby disclaims any responsibility for them.

Any people depicted in stock imagery provided by Thinkstock are models, and such images are being used for illustrative purposes only. Certain stock imagery © Thinkstock.

ISBN: 978-1-5127-1003-8 (sc)

Library of Congress Control Number: 2015913770

Print information available on the last page.

WestBow Press rev. date: 9/28/2015

Contents

Prologue

My road to this place, at this time in my life and for this moment, has given me good reason to write this booklet. In the Bible, there are precepts that pertain to the state of man and the way of life. This booklet derives from a spiritual perspective, from personal experiences and from the scriptures. Please understand that through this publication I aim to lift Jesus a little higher and a little higher. He has done a wonderful job of taking care of me. To paraphrase a song the late Rev. James Cleveland sang: "If anyone should write my life's story, tell them Jesus is the best thing that ever happened to me." Indeed this is my testimony. It is my hope that this little booklet, along with your Bible, will help you to meditate and remember some vital points about the practices of Christianity.

After going through several rough storms earlier in my life, I made a promise to the Lord that I would serve Him for the balance of my days. There were times when I stumbled, but God's amazing grace kept me afloat. One night long ago, I had a bitter sweet dream. Little did I know then that this dream signified a calling on my life. Later, I discovered it to be a vision; it continues to reveal itself through individuals.

In the dream I was standing on the west bank looking down at people in a valley of quicksand. Jesus, in all of His splendor and glory, was standing on the east bank facing me and looking down at the same people in the valley of quicksand, too. As a young lady the meaning did not resonate with my spirit, but the images remained. Years later while teaching bible study at a jail, the Lord spoke to my spirit and revealed to me that some of the people I saw in the valley of quicksand included members of the incarcerated population.

"Quicksand" is a word that is seldom used by this generation but it is still in the Lord's vocabulary. Quicksand is a mixture, to a certain level, of water and very soft sand that is incapable of holding any weight. Therefore, one is unable to stand on it without sinking; as fast as one foot is lifted, the other one sinks down. It is reasonable to say that many people, although moving, are sinking under their own weight. Metaphorically speaking, they are in quicksand.

The present system in America has this group of people boxed in with laws, rules and regulations. Criminal background checks are routine for virtually every worthwhile endeavor designed to enhance one's progress. Rap sheets are a mighty force to deal with now; they negatively impact one's credit relative to employment, housing, loans and virtually every aspect of citizenship in general.

The remedy I offer, to inmates and to any others in quicksand mode, is very simple: **Jesus Christ is the answer**. He has allowed the incarcerated to be placed in a position where they will have to lean and depend on Him for support. Jesus is the one who can work on the minds of people and change their attitudes as well as their perspectives. Through faith, He will open doors, where there is no door; He will make a way, out of no way, and he will put His people in a position where he can attend to their needs. *"Delight thyself also in the Lord; and He shall give thee the desires of thine heart."* (**Psalm 37:4**)

My vision allowed me to develop my relationship with Jesus Christ by leading me into the work of prison ministry. For more than a decade, I worked with the jail and prison ministry at my church. There is a need to be very careful with this ministry, so one must get accustomed to speaking or teaching without a microphone and most times without chairs. It all depends on the given area. If lessons are taught in the gym, nothing is facilitated, just the floor and four walls. If lessons are taught in the cafeteria, then tables and benches are present but they are of steel and they are immobile. Every time I went to a penal facility and taught, **the Lord amplified my voice**. We could hear my voice bouncing off the walls as it penetrated to the cells.

For inmates to "come to church," as they referred to it, was also a privilege. If an inmate misbehaved in jail, the privilege was taken away. One day as we passed by a cell door with a small window in it, the inmate knocked to get my attention. I looked at him and he simply said, "I heard what you said." That comment was music to my ears. Please note that there is no such thing as acoustics at these facilities. It is very hard to be heard. If the Lord doesn't amplify one's voice, most times the teaching is in vain. My amplified voice was and is only for an incarcerated population.

Prior to my days with jail and prison ministry, I was living in a different state but still had contacts in Florida, my home state. An officer to whom I was introduced asked me to give a workshop at one of the churches in Florida. The Holy Spirit showered us with such blessings until all participants thoroughly enjoyed it. I was blown away by the end results.

While riding home alone and rejoicing with the Lord, The Holy Spirit spoke to me in my language and with a voice I had not heard previously. The voice, a beautiful, exquisite sound, came up out of my stomach and penetrated through my ears. Then the voice said, **"You also have the gift of exhortation."** It left quickly. I said, "Come back here," and I did not hear another word from Him. The voice was a complete reversal from normalcy because spoken words come to our ears from without; but this voice came to my ears from within.

The Lord knew that I would not have ever recognized this gift, so He spoke to me on a level where I understood Him and I heard Him clearly. He stated that, **"You also have the gift of exhortation."** This meant that I have other gifts. The Holy Spirit knew that I was studying the gifts and had a profound interest in them. I am still intrigued by those gifts, especially, discerning of spirits. The endowed gifts have created within me a great hunger for God's Word and outreach ministries.

I am fascinated by the power of His Word and the knowledge that all it requires is belief. The physical manifestation of His presence in His Word is mind-boggling, as the Word is so alive! Those who serve Him come to love it, internalize it, taste it and see it at work. Nothing can separate God from His Word. I understand what David meant when he declared, *"O taste and see that the Lord is good."* (**Psalm 34:8**)

Chronologically, I have lived my three score and ten plus. Grace and mercy are with me for the rest of my days and "*I will dwell in the house of the Lord for ever,*" as Psalm 23 says. Like many of you, I could go on and on about the goodness of the Lord; however, I have said all of this for you to see the integrity of my soul. I challenge you to try God, believe His Word and let faith become a lifestyle as you develop a relationship with Jesus Christ. Select some of God's promises that speak to your heart, memorize them, recite them often until you taste the goodness and then act on them. Practice them by applying the principles to your everyday life. Sit back and watch how the Lord will take over by leading and guiding you. Remember that your faith will activate the scriptures. We pray that the remainder of your journey will be a better one as you enjoy the fullness of the Gospel.

---Helen Baker-Britt,
aka, "The Exhorter"

Introduction

And I, if I be lifted up from the earth,
will draw all men unto me.

John 12:32

This book is written in a simple style intended for all to understand. The text utilizes Scriptures to substantiate concepts, thoughts, and opinions. All Scriptures quoted in this booklet are from the King James Bible. The purpose of this book is to create a world of love and kindness. Love and kindness are two small but central ingredients that make a big difference in society. You can manifest love and kindness by rendering service. Rendering service, by serving in ministries and by lifting up Jesus Christ a little higher through God's Word, magnifies love and kindness.

We know that the Father, Son and Holy Spirit are one. The momentum of ministry, discipleship and rendering service is one. Serving in ministries blesses you and allows you to bless others. Ministry is a vehicle whereby faith becomes a lifestyle as you develop a relationship with Jesus Christ. Ministry also brings forth lasting fruit through the practical application of Scriptures. *"For where two or three are gathered together in my name, there am I in the midst of them."* **(Matthew 18:20)** And, *"I can do all things through Christ which strengtheneth me."* **(Philippians 4:13)**

This book could be considered as a primer for matured Christians; yet, it is incumbent upon matured Christians to teach the younger generation. *"But speak thou the things which become sound doctrine: That the **aged men** be sober, grave, temperate, sound in faith, in charity, in patience. The **aged women** likewise, that they be in behavior as becometh holiness, not false accusers, not given to much wine, teachers of good things; That they may teach the young women to be sober, to love their husbands, to love their children, To be discreet, chaste, keepers at home, good, obedient to their own husbands, that the word of God be not blasphemed. Young men likewise exhort to be sober minded."* **(Titus 2:1-6)**

How can a basic booklet be considered relevant for this generation? It becomes relevant to every generation, as long as the fullness of the Gospel has not been manifested. "Fullness of the Gospel" simply means that the majority of the spiritual gifts as highlighted in the Bible are not utilized in the majority of our churches. So as we progress into the 21st Century, new and old concepts are claiming and reclaiming arbitrary places in our society; but always bear in mind that the Bible is alive and Jesus Christ is alive and well, too.

A Ghanaian Proverb states *"The ruin of a nation begins in the homes of its people."* This proverb speaks volumes to a ton of problems in our society. What are some problems that tend to erode and dilute our value system?

- Too many people are stuck in "quicksand" and don't know how to get out because they are spiritually void.
- This generation has compromised the gospel to an extreme and many don't fully understand the true meaning of Christianity.
- False prophets, behaviors and lifestyles convey mixed-messages.

These topics speak to the heart of the matter, although others could have been added to the list.

How do we cope with this ever-changing world and the escalation of sin? When we take a look at what is going on today, there is an urgent need for many to develop a relationship with Jesus Christ. Reflecting on the spiritual, through my eyes as an elder, this is how I see the world today, tomorrow and beyond with a focus primarily on Jesus Christ.

"Too holy for any earthly good" is a common saying among some folks. *"But we are all as an unclean thing, and all our righteousnesses are as filthy rags."* **(Isaiah 64:6a)** Therefore, a review is always in order. Usually before a quiz or test, the instructor gives a review. And some may consider this text a review. In addition to being a refresher course, this booklet will also help those unfamiliar with Christian doctrine and the way in which it supports Christianity. Further, this booklet will help lukewarm Christians who need to be energized for the business of kingdom building. There is something in here for most people, even if it is repetitious.

I have observed that too many people have religion in the head rather than in the heart. They have forgotten that we are about kingdom building. Within the economy of ministry, and with the aid of the Holy Spirit, this is how I see Christianity today. So wake up, Church! It is time for more outreach ministries!

Jesus said, *And other sheep I have, which are not of this fold: them also I must bring, and they shall hear my voice; and there shall be one fold, and one shepherd.* **(John 10:16)**

ONE

Ministry

*Go your ways: behold, I send you forth
as lambs among wolves.*

Luke 10:3

To follow Christ is to continue **His Ministry.** Ministry will take participants to a place of prosperity by being a blessing to others due to role reversal. The word "ministry" tells Christians that you are servants of God; called to be empowered by His Word; inspired by the Holy Spirit to do His Will; and spiritually, offer encouragement to the 'least of these' while on this Christian journey. Experience and empirical data have proven that the happiest people are those who do the most for others, Our Lord is on a recruitment mission and only the strong will survive *"Even so faith, if it hath not works, is dead, being alone."* **(James 2:17)** This booklet is a guide to highlight the importance of being

1

a servant and enjoying the fullness of the Gospel. We serve a Holy God. He is merciful and loving and his standards are absolute. God's Word remains unchanged. The mystery of ministry is intertwined with the activation of His Word. Ministry is about the glory of God. Every true believer is anointed by the Holy Spirit. With this power comes spiritual gifts for the purpose of ministry. Ministry simply means to be used by God to help others, especially, those in need. Giving a donation to missionaries is not quite enough; you must do something with your spiritual gift to make a significant difference in the world. As you revisit God's Plan of Salvation and the tenets of faith, be reminded that His love for you is so great until mediocrity is not an option. He requires your best.

The time has come for the church to realize that it is a new day! We are the 21st Century Church. In the fullness of time, *"And we know that all things work together for good to them that love God, to them who are the called according to his purpose."* **(Romans 8:28)** Now is the time to implement Jesus' model of leadership.

- He asked for volunteers, "Follow Me"
- From the volunteer list, twelve (12) came forth
- When volunteerism came to a standstill, He implemented the draft system

- He drafted seventy (70) others and sent them forth in pairs of two

"After these things the Lord appointed other seventy also, and sent them two and two before his face into every city and place, whither he himself would come. Therefore said he unto them, The harvest truly is great, but the labourers are few: pray ye therefore the Lord of the harvest, that he would send forth labourers into his harvest. Go your ways: behold, I send you forth as lambs among wolves." **(Luke 10:1-3)**

Today, I think the average church, ratio-wise, has a small number of people who are really doing what the Lord expects for Christians to be doing. I would suggest that it is time to put the draft system in place. By implementing the draft system, an organizational chart using alphabets, zip codes or any method that is user-friendly is needed for the 21st Century Church. The process includes asking for volunteers with known spiritual gifts. If volunteerism doesn't work, implement the draft system. **Boldly announce that pew-sitting is not an option and will not be tolerated in God's House, unless you are physically, and mentally challenged**.

Jesus is serious about ministry. If you are a pastor and the majority of your members are pew-sitters, this book will serve a distinct purpose for your congregation because it focuses on Outreach Ministries. Most members love strong leadership, especially, when it is in line with God's Word. If you are a pew-sitter, this book will definitely motivate you to see the light.

The Holy Spirit has shared that Christians are in the minority in God's House and most of us already know that to be a fact. *"For every tree is known by his own fruit."* **(Luke 6:44a)** The church has detoured from the straight and narrow. We must bring people back to the foot of the cross. Like it or not, most church goers need to be converted in order to become Christians. Jesus answered and said unto Nicodemus, *"Verily, verily, I say unto thee, Except a man be born again, he cannot see the kingdom of God."* If you don't get it right voluntarily, there will come a day when you will be forced to get it right.

It is incumbent upon Christians to make this a better world before the **Second Coming.** Our Father always warns his people before judgment as documented by Noah's preaching. Because He loves us so, He wants us to join Him in Paradise for eternity. Just think how marvelous and wonderful it will be to have a better world. When all of the churches get busy with ministries—helping people, lifting Jesus and sharing God's Word—your town, city, state, and our nation will be wholesome places in which to live. And later, when we all get to Heaven, what a time, what a time, we will have as we shout and rejoice with our Savior!

As a footnote, know that while you are doing well; expect some wolves to show up. **Just say, "In the name of Jesus, get thee behind me Satan," and keep it moving.**

Beloved, believe not every spirit, but try the spirits whether they are of God: because many false prophets are gone out into the world. **(I John 4:1)**

TWO

Jesus Is Serious About Ministry

The Bible must be taught and applied; not taught and denied

Ministry is that part of Christianity which relates to being practical, proactive and pertinent to needs, circumstances and situations of people. It requires us to be kind and to love one another. Extending kindness will draw people to Christ. Ministry is the heart and soul of Christianity. Being faithful to one's calling and enjoying the fullness of the Gospel requires ministry.

Jesus was motivated to help people in pain and He understood pain. Isaiah described him as a man of sorrows and acquainted with grief. Ministry was on His mind. Without any hesitation, Jesus sent Dives straight to Hell for being unkind to Lazarus and not sharing his resources.

"And there was a certain beggar named Lazarus, which was laid at his gate, full of sores. And desiring to be fed with the crumbs which fell from the rich man's table: moreover the dogs came and licked his sores. And it came to pass, that the beggar died, and was carried by the angels into Abraham's bosom: the rich man also died, and was buried. And in hell he lift up his eyes, being in torments, and seeth Abraham afar off, and Lazarus in his bosom. And he cried and said, Father Abraham, have mercy on me, and send Lazarus, that he may dip the tip of his finger in water, and cool my tongue; for I am tormented in this flame. But Abraham said, Son, remember that thou in thy lifetime receivedst thy good things. And likewise Lazarus evil things; but now he is comforted, and thou art tormented." **(Luke 16:20–25)**

By any stretch of the imagination, **Jesus is very serious about ministry and spiritual empowerment.** All Christians should be involved in one or more ministries. A sample list of suggested ministries is included in this text to encourage participation. Most Christians could and should suggest many more ministries. Ministries, in place by name only in some churches, need committed and diligent workers. Therefore, the appeal to all pew-sitters is: Help make this world a better place in which to live. *"For he hath said, I will never leave thee, nor forsake thee."* *(Hebrews 13:5b)*

7

<u>Jesus is Explicit with Christians</u>

Jesus said, "For I was an hungred, and ye gave me meat: I was thirsty, and ye gave me drink: I was a stranger, and ye took me in: Naked, and ye clothed me: I was sick, and ye visited me: I was in prison, and ye came unto me. Then shall the righteous answer him, saying, Lord, when saw we thee an hungred, and fed thee? or thirsty, and gave thee drink? When saw we thee a stranger, and took thee in? or naked, and clothed thee? Or when saw we thee sick, or in prison and came unto thee? And the King shall answer and say unto them, Verily I say unto you, inasmuch as ye have done it unto one of the least of these my brethren, ye have done it unto me. "Then shall he say also unto them on the left hand, Depart from me, ye cursed, into everlasting fire, prepared for the devil and his angels: For I was an hungred and ye gave me no meat: I was thirsty, and ye gave me no drink: I was a stranger, and ye took me not in: naked, and ye clothed me not: sick, and in prison; and ye visited me not. Then shall they also answer him, saying, Lord, when saw we thee an hungred, or athirst, or a stranger, or naked, or sick, or in prison, and did not minister unto thee? Then shall he answer them, saying Verily I say unto you, inasmuch as ye did it not to one of the least of these, ye did it not to me. And these shall go away into everlasting punishment: but the righteous into life eternal." **(Matt 25:35-46)**

On one occasion during His earthly mission, Jesus was trying to field His team, and a certain man came up to Him and said, Jesus, I will follow you wherever you go. Jesus sensed that this man wanted notoriety, so he said, "Foxes have holes, birds of the air have nests but the Son of man has nowhere to lay His head." As he continued His journey, He said to another man, "Follow Me." This man said, "Lord, suffer me first to go home and bury my father." Jesus said unto him, "Let the dead bury the dead: but you go and preach the Kingdom of God." Another man said unto Jesus, "Lord I will follow thee but first let me go home and bid the family farewell." Jesus said unto him, "No man putting his hand to the plough and looking back is fit for the Kingdom of God." **(Luke 9:57–62)** This is somewhat paraphrased but the essence is the same. It further proves that Jesus is serious about ministry. Excuses and distractions are unacceptable reasons for failing to employ ministry. There is a dire need for us to catch a glimpse of Jesus' vision and carry on in a mighty way. So let's put aside idiosyncrasies, lift each other up in love and prepare to meet Jesus when He comes.

For we brought nothing into this world, and it is certain we can carry nothing out. **(I Timothy 6:7)**

THREE

Spiritual Gifts

**Teach me to do thy will;
for thou art my God...
(Psalms 143:10a)**

The church is responsible for equipping the saints for
<u>service</u> and building the Body of Christ. Service itself
is a balm to both the spirit and the body. The Holy
Spirit gives spiritual gifts to each Christian for the
sole purpose of ministry. Spiritual gifts correlate with
ministries. As singing is to the choir and teaching is to
teaching, so it is with all spiritual gifts. One must act
on the Holy Spirit's <u>calling</u> to fulfill his purpose. A
spiritual gift is referred to as one's calling. **The pain
that reaches you most deeply is your calling,
and yet, it inspires your soul to an exhilarating
high**. If your spiritual gift is not known, a born again
experience might be in order; you might have to go by

the cross to pick up your redemption papers. Continue to pray, ask God to come into your heart, forgive you of your sins and save your soul.

Every member of the human race has some sort of natural talent. Natural talents may or may not carry over and become spiritual gifts. A spiritual conversion normally converts talents into spiritual gifts but not always; sometimes this conversion adds new gifts to Christians. Gifts equip the saints to fulfill their purpose through service for the building of the body of Jesus Christ. Many gifts have not been given their proper places in the church making this generation somewhat clueless about their existence and purpose.

The Body of Jesus Christ is one blood. Each cell receives nourishment from the same blood. All Christians have been brought into the Body through the blood of our Lord and Savior, Jesus Christ. By definition, spiritual gifts are the life blood of the church. They were put in place to help make this journey easier and to render service with power.

A composite listing of spiritual gifts includes the following: Administration, Apostle, Discerning of Spirits, Evangelist, Exhortation, Faith, Giving, Healing, Helps, Interpretation, Knowledge, Leadership, Mercy, Miracles, Pastor, Prophecy, Service, Teaching, Tongues,

and Wisdom. This list came from 1 Corinthians 12, Romans 12, and Ephesians 4. There are a few other gifts that are located in isolated areas of the Bible and not included above.

Some Perks for being obedient and becoming a willing worker:

- *Delight thyself also in the Lord; and he shall give thee the desires of thine heart.* **(Psalm 37:4)**
- *If ye abide in me, and my words abide in you, ye shall ask what ye will, and it shall be done unto you.* **(John 15:7)**
- *But my God shall supply all your need according to his riches in glory by Christ Jesus.* **(Philippians 4:19)**
- *Bring ye all the tithes into the storehouse, that there may be meat in mine house, and prove me now herewith, saith the LORD of hosts, if I will not open you the windows of heaven, and pour you out a blessing, that there shall not be room enough to receive it.* **(Malachi 3:10)**

Do you see where I am going with this? Being a willing worker will <u>activate</u> the promises of God in your life. Just think. If all the Christians in the world would become willing workers, this would be a beautiful world. Folks, I don't care how you slice it; we are stuck with each other. Let's open our hearts, link arms and be about our Father's business. Our Heavenly Father wants to spiritually promote us to a higher level but it can only be done through ministry. Effective ministry will bring to the Church lasting fruit and that fruit will bear additional fruit, and more fruit will keep coming so that the church lives on...and on...and forever.

And he gave some, apostles; and some, prophets; and some, evangelists; and some, pastors and teachers; for the perfecting of the saints, for the work of the ministry, for the edifying of the body of Christ. **(Ephesians 4:11-12)**

FOUR

Discipleship

**Thou wilt keep him in perfect peace,
whose mind is stayed on thee.**

(Isaiah 26:3a)

Jesus said, "Follow Me"

While Jesus Christ was discharging His mission on earth, He taught by precept and example. His teaching was immediate and direct. It fascinated people's imagination to the point that many listened. His leadership style was simplistic, nurturing and instructive. Jesus himself came as a servant but He was a mover and a shaker. He confronted His enemies, defended the poor, performed miracles, healed the sick and broken hearted, ministered to the needy, taught and preached to the multitudes; and still He had time to train and make disciples. Discipleship is a lifestyle that says one has accepted the

14

teaching of Jesus Christ and is willing to follow Him, learn of Him and spread the Gospel throughout all nations.

The Church is called to make disciples and that takes a significant amount of time. Jesus took the time and taught disciples for about two or three years. His leadership style is a very good model. Disciples are rooted and grounded in the Word. They have a solid foundation built on a commitment to Christianity. They possess a profundity associated with having a relationship with Jesus. Disciples get things done in a timely manner because discipleship is a vital part of ministry. They are like sheep who know the voice of their Shepherd and they follow only Him. *"My sheep hear my voice, and I know them, and they follow me."* **(John 10:27)** The Holy Spirit empowers disciples to faithfully execute their duty to lift Christ a little higher as they teach and walk the Christian walk. I pray for today's disciples to remember that you are following Jesus, not man. He is your Shepherd.

Mission for Discipleship:

To exemplify holiness and the fundamental principles of the Cross, Christ and the Church through spiritual empowerment with a posture of spreading the Gospel as a way of life.

Discipleship embraces these values:

S... See the Future (vision)

E... Empower self and others

R... Re-visit basic Christian principles

V... Value relationships

E... Encourage positive thinking

- Prayer (***Pray without ceasing***)
- Service
- Fasting (optional) and living by faith
- Follow-up with new Christians by making the initial contact within one week
- Love sharing God's goodness; walk with new Christians for at least one year

Walking with new Christians for at least a year is essential to discipleship. Some may require a longer period of time, for building a solid foundation in Christianity is time consuming. There is a need for this generation to understand fully what Christ meant when He said, 'Follow me." The Bible says, one must deny himself, take up his cross and follow Jesus. "Then said Jesus unto his disciples, *If any man will come after me, let him deny himself, and take up his cross, and follow me."* (**Matthew 16:24**)

Our 'values system' has gotten lost in the casualness of 'anything goes.' As aforementioned, we have lost our way and it is time for the lost sheep to return to the fold and bring others along. Therefore, let's proactively embrace discipleship with heart and love. Begin anew by evangelizing and strengthening the Body of Christ through His Word, worship, praise and service. Power, preparation and pursuit are words to internalize as we continue this journey called life; a journey from earth to heaven. **Heaven is a prepared place for a prepared people.** *Jesus said, "I go to prepare a place for you."* (**John 14:2b**) Service is a form of preparation.

Jesus vividly portrayed servant-hood as a way of life. Service is the price we pay for saying, "Good Morning." My Christian elders referred to it as "sending up your timber." Now is the right time to reach down and bring others up, as a manifestation of the love of Jesus.

I was glad when they said unto me, Let us go into the house of the Lord. (**Psalm 122:1**)

17

FIVE

Pew-Sitters

They profess that they know God;
but in works they deny him...

(Titus 1:16a)

God holds our tomorrows; don't abandon the chance to
serve Him. I see Titus 1:16a as describing pew-sitters.
Many may not count pew-sitting as denying God. But
the WORD says that it is denial. As I see it, there are few
Christians who are engaged in witnessing for the Lord.
So logic would dictate that there are many Christians
who are "pew-sitters." The challenge for the Church
today is: **HOW TO MOVE THE PEW SITTERS
TO THE HARVEST FIELD.** Jesus declared that,
"The harvest truly is plenteous, but the labourers are few."
(Matthew 9:37) The Kingdom of God is seeking
willing workers to witness to the world that salvation

18

is free but it comes only through Jesus Christ. What makes this a hard task for most Christians?

- It requires divine power to transform the minds of people; therefore it forces church-goers to get saved and ask the Lord to come into their hearts and forgive them of their sin.
- One must study the Bible in order to rightly divide the Word of truth.
- A relationship with Jesus Christ must be developed.
- You must give of yourself and share your resources.
- The four walls of the church serve as a safety net for pew-sitters.
- Too many Christians are spiritually lazy and the word LOVE has not resonated with their proactive spirit.

A classic example of taking the first step is the use of debit and credit cards. Upon receiving a new card, one must first activate it before use. And so it is with ministry. The first step is to activate your faith in the ministry and the Lord will help with the other steps. As the ministry grows in your spirit, then David's word will speak to your heart, *"I was glad when they said unto me, Let us go into the house of the LORD."* **(Psalm 122:1)**

God's Word is alive and well but sitting in the pews will not activate it. That is why faith without works is dead. **We must <u>do something</u> in the lives of people.**

The mission of the 21ˢᵗ Century Church is to focus on the harvest field. (A generic format for the future church is included in *Chapter 7*.) The message of this book is worthy of notice; although repetitious in content, there is nothing new under the sun. This proves that Christianity and salvation are just simple acts of faith. When taught, even a little child understands that Jesus loves him; so there is nothing complicated about Christianity. We aim to move the pew-sitters to the harvest field through outreach ministries, discipleship and service. My philosophy is aligned to David McGee, pastor of The Bridge church in central North Carolina. McGee said, "We should be more concerned with reaching the lost, rather than pampering the saved."

And whatsoever ye do in word or deed, do all in the name of the Lord Jesus, giving thanks to God and the Father by him. **(Colossians 3:17)**

Put on the whole armour of God, that ye may be able to stand against the wiles of the devil. **(Ephesians 6:11)**

SIX

Hope

Now the God of hope fill you with all joy and peace in believing...
(Romans 15:13)

A Higher Hope will propel your mind to a place of peace, enrich your posture, and lift your spirit. *"Now the God of hope fill you with all joy and peace in believing, that ye may abound in hope, through the power of the Holy Ghost."* **(Romans 15:13)** I cannot think of a better definition of Hope than this popular one: **"Hope sees the invisible, feels the intangible, and achieves the impossible."**

Continuing this journey will be an uphill climb if Jesus is not a part of the equation. He died for our sins so that we would not have to make this journey alone. Take notice of the major changes that are taking place on earth: the crime element is increasing, the lack of gun control is devastating, new diseases are surfacing, evil is all around us, the Church has narrowed its perspective, and the weather is making a profound statement. It is worth noting that, despite what meteorologists are saying about the weather conditions, God is warning the entire world: "Jesus is on His way, so get your house in order." The conditions I have referred to might easily be classified as pestilences.

"This know also, that in the last days perilous times shall come...." **(II Timothy 3:1)** *"And Jesus answered and said unto them, Take heed that no man deceive you. For many shall come in my name, saying, I am Christ; and shall deceive many. And ye shall hear of wars and rumours of wars: see that ye be not troubled: for all these things must come to pass, but the end is not yet. For nation shall rise against nation, and kingdom against kingdom: and there shall be famines, and pestilences, and earthquakes in divers places. All these are the beginning of sorrows."* **(Matthew 24:4-8)**

There is a void that needs to be filled by helping people to get rid of selfishness, the pursuit of instant gratification, greed and other shortcomings that are unpleasant in the sight of God. I strongly suggest replacing these negatives with the Fruit of the Spirit: Love, joy, peace, longsuffering, gentleness, goodness, faith, meekness and temperance. The overall strategy features KINDNESS and HOPE as one way to bring others into the sheepfold. Good deeds will keep hope alive and encourage Christians to assert more energy toward helping others. This is because, spiritually, the giver's reward is far greater than the recipient's gift. HOPE is looking forward to a better day and a better world, as well as to the Second Coming of Jesus Christ.

Now faith is the substance of things hoped for, the evidence of things not seen. (**Hebrews 11:1**)

SEVEN

The Contemporary / Future Church

It is amazing how the world is forever changing. The evolution of the Church is undergoing a major change, too, with a focus on the younger generation. Many larger churches are trying hard to keep the youth engaged. Smaller churches are having a bit of catching up to do. Many have not figured out how to evangelize and retain this younger generation. I think smaller churches need a major overhaul with a keen eye on ministries. If a change is not imminent, smaller churches will soon be out of business, because the future church is based on today's youth.

So the best prescriptions are to be about the business of helping people and concentrate on spiritual empowerment, rather than sitting in church every Sunday soaking up one's salvation. This guide comes to help churches fulfill the Will of God. It is incumbent upon Christians to be movers and shakers rather than pew-sitters.

Previously, a friend shared with me information that the Holy Spirit revealed to her. She requested action. I sat on it for about five or six years, wondering how to convey such a profound message effectively. This book was chosen to unveil what the Sunday Worship Service will look like in the years to come.

The following changes will take place during the normal Sunday morning worship. **The Future Church/ Worship Services will look like this:**

First Sundays... Traditional service with sermon and probably communion; the Lord's Supper Ministry is in charge of communion. The first Sunday service is the same or similar to what is taking place now.

Second Sundays... Suggested, pre-planned topical discussions that are biblically based will take place at this worship service. Congregation and community will submit topics that interest them to the leadership committee. Committee will evaluate and submit topics that are needed for spiritual growth.

Third Sundays... The entire membership will be asked to engage and participate in outreach ministries;

the community will send needs requests to designated ministries for consideration; these ministries will select the projects and schedule everything. Instead of worship service in the church, rather, the congregation will gather at the church for prayer and disperse to the community and render service at varies sites. Larger churches will require a defined organizational chart to accommodate the membership and/or participants.

Fourth Sundays... Quiet Prayer and Bible Study or reading at home, church, alone or with family and/or in small groups. This is a very good time to engage in devotion with the Lord through the Blessed Quietness Ministry.

Fifth Sundays... This Sunday was not included in the revelation. The congregation may opt to do whatever is feasible for spiritual empowerment.

Do you know the difference between *worship and service*? Sometimes they are written together as *worship service.* In layman's terminology *worship* is intense love and admiration for God and *service* is volunteer employment to those in need. Together, it is a gathering of people to sing, pray and participate in a *worship service* for the glory of God; commonly referred to as going to church. Going to church in most cases embodies worship. There are a few in-house ministries that are associated with *worship service*; but the majority of ministries are outreach. *"And now abideth faith, hope, charity, these three; but the greatest of these is charity."* **(I Corinthians 13:13**) The Holy Spirit guides many Christians to charity, as they go about the business of helping people.

There is real power in the name of Jesus that comes through by way of the Holy Spirit. Trust the Lord. Keep your faith in Him and believe His Living Word. The Lord expects for us to be as busy as little ants in advancing the Kingdom of God because every Christian is a minister. As Christians, we should remember that the Lord calls us to:

- Worship Him
- Witness for Him
- And render service unto Him

The Holy Spirit also empowers us to forgive those who inflict pain and disobey the laws of the land by being abusive.

But the salvation of the righteous is of the Lord: He is their strength in the time of trouble. (Psalm 37:39)

EIGHT

Spiritual Fitness

Behold I show you a mystery: we shall not all be in darkness but we shall be in the knowledge of God. He is desirous of wholeness. Far too many people are suffering from broken spirits, broken relationships, broken hearts and broken bodies. In fact, we live in a broken world as evidenced by the internet, television and the news in general.

The process of healing begins with the individual. For the ultimate Healer is within each person. God has given each person a measure of faith. All you need is enough faith that is the size of a mustard seed. *"And Jesus said unto them, If ye have faith as a grain of mustard seed, ye shall say unto this mountain, Remove hence to yonder place; and it shall remove; and nothing shall be impossible unto you."* **(Matthew 17:20)**

Faith

"God hath dealt to every man the measure of faith."
(Romans 12:3b) You don't even have to be saved to enjoy the measure of faith; it is a gift at birth. When toddlers are learning to walk is an example of this. They fall down but they get back up, because they have the faith they will walk. You must take the first step. It is how you use your measure of faith that determines your destiny.

A deepening of faith or an increase of faith will come by way of works and storms. Faith is the greatest activator of the healing process. Without faith, serving God is ineffective. On several occasions Jesus said to the sick your faith hath made you whole. Too often people become too consumed with fear, the condition, rather that faith and healing. I have put together several spiritual prescriptions that may be used to assist with healing the mind, body and soul, in accordance with God's Will, coupled with a strong dosage of faith. Love, kindness, forgiveness, testimonies, prayer and Scriptures are all akin to ministry and healing. Remember, ministry is an awesome spiritual tool that all Christians are called to implement.

Standing on God's promises in faith helps to heal many physical conditions in accordance with His Will.

If the desired healing does not occur, you will become a better person spiritually. Prayer and the element of time will help you to overcome emotional deficiencies; and God's WORD will heal the wounded soul. Please note that Jesus never told the sick to go to bed; instead, at times He would extend his hand and say, "…Behold… Arise… Go thy way…"

"Behold, thou art made whole: sin no more, lest a worst thing come unto thee." **(John 5:14)** *"I say unto thee, <u>Arise</u>, and take up thy bed, and <u>go thy way</u> into thine house."* **(Mark 2:11)** *"And he said unto her, For this saying <u>go thy way</u>; the devil is gone out of thy daughter."* **(Mark 7:29)**

When all fails, take inventory of self, make sure you are being honest with God through confessions and be absolutely sure that obedience is your mantra. The Lord meets people on their own individual level. What will work for one person may not work for someone else. The bottom line to any healing prescription is your level of faith. So be absolutely sure about your belief; many times it encompasses more than what we think. Don't be deceived by the enemy in thinking you have it made ('it' meaning all of that). Repent, surrender all and keep looking up. If a healing doesn't take place, continue to trust in Him; **God's Grace is sufficient for you.**

<u>Kindness</u>

Let the good be so pronounced that even your enemies will applaud you. Any form of **kindness** is a Godly act and a healing agent. A portion of our daily activities should be predicated on <u>kindness,</u> as we are called to minister to the needs of people. You need to walk in the Truth for that is where Jesus walks. Studying the WORD and sharing God's goodness will help to bring Salvation to others. Kindness and love walk together. Know that love is not love until it is given away. By the Spirit of God, I challenge you to be about kingdom building and lifting Jesus a little higher in kindness and love.

Spiritual Fitness for the mind, body and spirit: read Scriptures aloud

<u>First Prescription</u>: The first line of defense should be to feed the mind a daily diet of healing Scriptures, coupled with the power of great faith, praise and thanksgiving; *"and with His stripes we are healed."* (**Isaiah 53:5b**) *"Now unto him that is able to do exceeding abundantly above all that we ask or think, according to the power that worketh in us."* **(Ephesians 3:20)**

Second Prescription: Through faith, speak to your mountain, pray often and engage in a fast at least one day a week. *"Death and life are in the power of the tongue"…* (**Proverbs 18:21a**)

Third Prescription*: "Is any among you afflicted? Let him pray."* (**James 5:13a**)

Fourth Prescription:*"Is any sick among you? Let him call for the elders of the church; and let them pray over him, anointing him with oil in the name of the Lord. And the prayer of faith shall save the sick, and the Lord shall raise him up; and if he have committed sins, they shall be forgiven him."* (**James 5: 14 & 15**)

Fifth Prescription:A mixture of any of the above coupled with a positive attitude and great faith.*"For we walk by faith, not by sight."* (**2 Corinthian 5:7**)

Sixth Prescription: This is for hemorrhaging. *"And when I passed by thee, and saw thee, polluted in thine own blood, I said unto thee when thou wast in thy blood, Live; Yea, I said unto thee when thou wast in thy blood, Live."* (**Ezekiel 16:6**)

Seventh Prescription:*"If my people, which are called by my name, shall humble themselves, and pray, and seek my face, and turn from their wicked ways; then will I hear from* *heaven, and will forgive their sin, and will heal their land."* **(II Chronicles 7:14)**

Eighth Prescription: To help fight Alzheimer's disease, use the prayers of faith and the power of God's Word: Memorize and recite Bible verses often for inspiration and action. God is no shorter than His Word. You must keep the brain active daily. *"For with God all things are possible."* **(Mark 10:27b)**

God has the last word. Like Abraham, put your trust in Him, expect Him to incline His ear and hear your prayers. If any type of brokenness exists with you, try hard to get well for it takes able bodies to be a fighting soldier. Faith in God's Word is a vital ingredient for healing. One cannot separate God from His Word; they are one and the same. *"In the beginning was the Word, and the Word was with God, and the Word was God."* **(John 1:1)**

"But ye are a chosen generation, a royal priesthood, an holy nation, a peculiar people; that ye should shew forth the praises of him who hath called you out of darkness into the marvellous light." **(1 Peter 2:9)**

As you peruse the suggested listing of ministries, many are the regular ministries which have been in churches for years. Others have been added to give Christians some additional choices. Now is the time

33

for you to add some to this list, too. Many outreach ministries lend themselves to helping others as well as empowering self. Several functions of the listed ministries are overlapping or similar in nature. Ministries should be tailored to fit one's congregation and community at large. An interrelationship between spiritual gifts, ministry, disciplineship and rendering service are necessary for the advancement of God's Kingdom.

Spiritual Gifts help Christians to stay purpose-driven and maintain the energy level that is required to do God's work. As a servant, you extend kindness to others and acknowledge the fact that God sent you to perform the given tasks. After all, we are His mouthpiece, arms, hands, legs and feet; for we represent the glory of God. Walking with new converts for a lengthy period of time is godly. The leadership style of Jesus Christ is an excellent model for us to follow. **Being a servant is the highest form of leadership.** Discipleship and rendering service are the active legs of ministry; which simply means that the needs of people are being met.

And why call ye me, Lord, Lord, and do not the things which I say? **(Luke 6:46)**

34

Epilogue

The Holy Spirit has done a great job of teaching me. Many times it was through trial and error and other times it has been at three o'clock in the morning. I became a Christian during my teenage years and have maintained my relationship with Christ ever since. Of course there were times when I made a detour; but the hand of God guided me and put me back on the straight and narrow.

Throughout my life I have encountered a number of challenges. When I was younger and having babies, I prayed often. During that time the Rh-negative factor was an issue to deal with; I was a victim. My prayer was for my children to be spared the blood issue that plagued their mother. My prayers were answered; I gave birth to healthy children.

Many years ago my father was diagnosed with cancer and that was before modern medicine came on the scene. I asked the Lord to heal my dad. He healed him. I promised to serve God for the rest of my life.

Dad lived to be ninety-one. I am so thankful that our Heavenly Father is no shorter than His Word.

Later in life, my husband passed away. While he was ill, I retired from the public school system. The very next year, I packed up everything and moved to a town where the only person I knew was me. I met new people, studied the Bible, developed and participated in ministry. **This place was my Mt Olivet.** After four years of studying, I moved to another state and began working again; this time at a college.

Several years later, I moved back home where my mother lived. I continued working at another college and became a participant with my church's jail and prison ministry. In assisting people in making changes in their lives, my primary goal was to advance the Kingdom of God.

I learned a lot from the incarcerated population and enjoyed every moment of it. I discovered a need while working in that ministry. Many of the younger generation did not buy or own a Bible. I began distributing Bibles to the incarcerated. It was that experience in ministry that helped develop the idea for this book.

Finally, I, like most people, did not want certain diseases to occur in my body. But guess what? All of them came rushing in, from breast cancer to, most recently, having a stroke. Today, I am able to say that the prayers of the righteous availeth much, so grace and mercy came along and rescued me.

Christianity is simply having a personal relationship with Jesus Christ. It is a one on one relationship. According to the television news, most people are tired of the hypocrisy that they see every day in some form or fashion. Hypocrisy is aggravating. But don't let it deter your relationship with Christ. Just remember that it is a tool of Satan. Rather than focusing on others, our primary duty is to remain obedient to God.

God has only one specific purpose for us, which is to be like His beloved Son. It is good to know that God is our help in every need; for He gives us power for each moment of our weakness. Often times in the storms of life, God gives us that extra push or shove needed to get the job done. Be reminded that God is a community of three, the Father, Son and Holy Spirit.

I am so thankful to my God for His amazing grace. As a result of doing the will of God, joy, happiness and peace are also my traveling companions. I believe that the highest attainment one can achieve in this world is to meet Jesus. Please tap into His everlasting power and enjoy the blessings He has for you.

Appendix

Suggested Church Ministries / Annotated Listing
Serve the Lord with gladness (Psalm 100:1a)

Adopt-A-Child... This ministry is similar to the foster parent and mentorship concepts. Adopt a needy child, informally. Needy refers to lacking in social skills, good physical health, academic achievement and/or any other missing attributes or essentials. Adopt means to assist with needed support to a child, without having him/her come to live in the home or to permanently adopt through legal procedures. Participation in this ministry blesses the Lord and you; the future church begins with children.

Adopt-A-Family Ministry... Same as above, except it is the entire family rather than one child. Look around your city and you will see that homelessness is prevalent. Many families could use a helping hand to get back on their feet, so let God's love prevail. Your generosity will be a mutual blessing as you become an earthly angel.

Adopt-A-School Ministry... To assist a school by filling needed voids. Minister to the needs of the school as a mutual venture and serve as a resource center by being supportive. Schools are always in need of volunteers. Thank faculty and staff with receptions, classroom materials, appreciation cards and other acts of kindness. Dedicate at least one Sunday annually to the school. Ask all to visit and give the school a donation.

Agape Foreign Missionary Ministry... Their gifts are used to minister to others, especially, those in another culture. They have resolved to serve rather than be served. They are a part of the earthly angels' culture. Members go to poor countries to help the needy and render unbelievable relief to the residents of those countries. The Holy Spirit equips them for this calling and He protects their well-being.

Amazing Grace Ministry... Folks that realize they are still here by the grace of God, knowing that He brought them through many atrocities in life. They are members of this ministry; their witness attests to the fact that God's grace is sufficient for them. So when all else fail, grace abounds. They know that Christians are connected by the **blood**, the **spirit** and **God's Amazing Grace.**

Archive and Heritage Ministry... Members are to collect, restore, organize and save information pertaining to the history of the Church. They are to establish a permanent library if one is not in place and information should be shared with children as well as adults.

Arts and Crafts ministry... Make this a little social hour for members to make arts and crafts. Add other niceties to the agenda that will give a little pizzazz to the meetings while continuing to stay focused. Donations are made to the church or a non-profit agency as items are sold.

Attendant's Ministry...Ushers should delicately enforce religious decorum for Church services. Ushers will recruit and train others with a focus on things being done in order, while creating a wholesome spiritual impression for the Lord. A spiritual design should be in place to make seating comfortable.

Baptismal Ministry...Prior to baptism, bond and share with new members some tidbits about this Christian journey. Assist with making preparation for baptism. Explain the "why" of baptism.

Beautification Ministry...(Interior and Exterior of Church) The Bride of Jesus should be looking good at all times and tastefully done. The House of Faith is the best looking house in the neighborhood; it represents the King of Kings. If not, membership should keep this as a job in progress.

Benevolent Ministry...Members with the gift of mercy usually participate in agape love activities. They are deeply involved with victims of unfortunate circumstances. Going beyond the call of duty to be kind and generous to people. Examples: The down-and-out, bereaved families, sick & shut-in, homeless, fire and storm victims, etc.

Bible Study Ministry...A regular diet of God's Word is a must at Church and at home. Studying the Bible enhances biblical astuteness and spiritual growth; there is a need for the church to establish small, neighborhood classes and intimate Bible study, outreach groups. This ministry will create worthwhile incentives and a spiritual climate to motivate people to study God's Word.

Blessed Quietness Ministry... The uniqueness of this ministry is that it only embraces one person (you, the reader of this document). So set aside a slot of time at least once per week to fellowship with the Lord in order to hear His voice. This devotion is imperative as you surrender the element of seclusion for communication purposes to solidify spiritual growth and a relationship with Jesus Christ.

Beautiful October Ministry... In some regions, this is the month of the year when the weather is perfect, the sky is blue, no clouds are present, the sun is bright and the leaves are turning into all kinds of beautiful colors. Plan an outdoor celebration to give God the glory for sharing His beauty with us. The cascades of turning leaves are breathtaking. Bring that same radiance in the church to add some excitement and help change those with negative attitudes.

Calendar and Events Ministry... Responsibilities include keeping a calendar of events for the Church coupled with initiating and scheduling events for the Church; also, making sure things are done decently and in order.

Campus Ministry...(College towns) An extra dosage of kindness goes a long ways with students away from home. The Church can be a vital force in their lives and should establish a viable relationship with students. Encourage active participation within the church and campus Bible study along with other campus activities by organizing a campus ministry on each college campus.

Cancer Survivor Ministry... Survivors are fully aware of the many challenges, prayers, and support they receive from each other. Nobody knows what it is like except the people who have been through the many ordeals of cancer. Support among members and non-members embrace friendship, prayer partners and the love for one another.

Career Education Ministry... Utilize members in the church and others from the community who are professionally associated with knowledge pertaining to careers. Teach children and young adults the value of education and choosing a career that relates to their abilities, interests and skills. Help them to find themselves and render services thereof.

Cell Group Ministry... This ministry recognizes that the church is the Body of Jesus Christ and it is as a living, growing organism. The cell groups vary in size depending on the size of the congregation. They are committed groups who are following the Shepherd by engaging in spiritual empowerment and evangelism. Their focus is on sharing the goodness of God through practical religion for the purpose of kingdom building.

Children's Church Ministry..."*Train up a child in the way he should go: and when he is old,* he *will not depart from it.*" **(Proverbs 22:6)** This is the future church. Spiritual development of children rests with the church. The children should be actively involved in this ministry. Children must take on leadership roles in their church, namely, deacons, trustees, ushers, choir, etc; all of this under the auspices of adult leadership and the Young Adult Ministry.

Church Assessment and Evaluation Ministry... Devise assessment forms to evaluate ministries; set a timeline for this process, keep records on the progress of each ministry, as well as their outcomes and projections. When needed, solicit and offer suggestions for improvement and make this information known to the leadership of the church.

Compassionate Listener and Telephone Ministry... Kindly listen patiently to those who have a need to vent their frustrations. It could be in person, by telephone and/or social media. Serving as a sounding board, at times, can be a preventative measure for anything an unclean spirit delivers. This is a good time to lift up Christ. When you think the Lord is not listening, He is right there and always hears your cries.

Cookies and Pies Ministry...A very good ministry for members who are homebound and unable to attend church. Some members are caregivers, some in wheelchairs, and yet, they want to be involved in ministry. Baking cookies and pies could be their thing of joy. These goodies may be given to new members as a welcome mat, to children who attend Sunday school and vacation Bible school, or shared with the homeless victims and others as a manifestation of God's love.

Coping with Diabetes Ministry... Members in this ministry will bond for the sake of coping with a disease that is detrimental. Also, they will serve as a support group by focusing on reversing diabetes through healthy diets, exercise and prayer.

Crossroads Ministry... This ministry affords one the opportunity to submit to corporate prayer, to articulate needs, to make some spiritual assessments and to establish guidelines for moving forward or choosing a road that leads to progress. This is a citadel for people at a crossroad who don't know which way to go. By sharing and collaborating with others who might have the same needs, it gives solace, and hopefully, good directions for accomplishing their mission.

Counseling Ministry... Members with the gift of wisdom, mature Christians and those with degrees in counseling should become members. They assist with conflicts and negative encounters; they advise as well as offer encouragement and solutions.

Count My Blessings Ministry... Be reminded that Jesus Christ counts everything; He even knows the number of hairs on your head. He counts your money too and knows all of your accounts. This is a one person ministry. Individually, each person will count and write down their blessings as often as necessary. With each new day there are new mercies, so this task will never end. Keeping a journal of your blessings will help to increase your faith and appreciate your purpose as serving others become a lifestyle.

Daughters of the King... The many storms that rage in the lives of these women have made them spiritually strong. They have taken Jesus as their closest friend by rejoicing and witnessing for Him. They share their wisdom with the younger women of the church and the community at large.

Dance and Drama Ministry... Spiritually, dance has become popular in churches today among the younger members. Moreover, portrayal of the birth, death, burial and resurrection of Jesus as well as biblical stories are integral parts of the drama department in many churches.

Diaconate Ministry...Commonly known as the Deacon Board; this Board consists of members with the gift of leadership. The word Diaconate simply means servant; it is used to encourage women to become deacons. Bear in mind that Jesus Christ died to remove all barriers and man came behind him and put them all up again. However, all power still rests in Him, not man. So women with this gift are encouraged to become members of this ministry.

Discerning of Spirits Ministry... The gift of discernment is unique in that members with this gift are able to discern unclean spirits when others are oblivious. They test the spirit by the spirit and have a keen ear for differentiating holiness from the unclean spirit of sounding brass and tinkling symbols. This helps the church to attend to unclean matters in a spiritual way and stay in a forward movement.

Discipleship Ministry... Jesus trained His disciples by walking, talking and teaching them as they followed Him. This ministry follows the same pattern. Deacons and church leaders will walk with new members for as long as necessary to encourage them and to share Christian values. It is a must for the church and leadership to nurture new converts and train new members.

Economic Empowerment Ministry... Keeping members informed of financial matters that are taking place in the world and encourage them to pray and invest is the purpose of this ministry. Also, a goal is to render encouragement to the church, as one unit, to invest in worthy projects to benefit mankind, such as, nursing homes, assisted living facilities, restaurants, schools, etc. Try to make a profit in order to have more money to give to the poor.

Education Ministry... Keeping the church in a reading mode is the primary goal for this ministry. Moreover, once per month, invite a medical doctor to talk about preventive measures on health issues; or others who will talk about relevant issues that will be helpful to the membership. Also, encourage young people to stay in school and empower them with the how, what and why of education.

Elders' Ministry... James 5:14 highlights Elders in a mighty way. This ministry may consist of some lay members, ministers, deacons and those who are spirit-filled. They are spiritual leaders in the church and normally few in number. Their effectiveness could be maximized by partnering with the prayer ministry.

Embracement Ministry... Sharing a passion to embrace something different is the focus for this ministry. It could be a good idea, a Psalm, a song, a prayer, a precept, a Bible verse, a book, a Sunday school lesson and anything that will help Christians to run this race with deliberate speed. Having faith in one or more of these positive elements will work wonders for believers.

Evangelism Ministry... This ministry is a divine calling. Those with an evangelism gift should fulfill this mission by sharing the gospel with unbelievers. In essence, it is about winning souls for Christ in a mighty way. The success of this gift is known through its attraction to the lost. In other words, it is a drawing card gift.

Exhortation ministry... Members with this gift add zest to the soulful life of the church because it is a divine calling also. Exhortation amplifies the Spirit and magnifies Jesus Christ through worship, prayers, songs, speeches and sermons. Words of comfort and encouragement to those in need of such services are an integral part of the Exhortation Ministry. Exhorters are always trying to lift Jesus higher as they encourage others to stay committed to the cause.

Faith Ministry... This type of faith is a spiritual gift. It includes those with the ability to discern the **Will** of God for the purpose of the church to move forward and exhort Jesus Christ. They know in their hearts that faith will move mountains, as they practice what they preach or teach daily. Faith is also a lifestyle that encompasses the way one thinks and acts.

Family Ministry... God ordained the family unit as a valuable vessel to perpetuate the church. Within this unit, love prevails and so it is in the church for God is love. The family and the home serve as the first training ground for the future church. The church is a community of believing families who are called to share their love and knowledge with the world.

Fellowship, Food & Fun Ministry... To provide, prepare, and serve food on specific occasions as a kind gesture or as a fellowship enhancement treat. Annual banquets, anniversaries, watch night services and many other events could be a recipient of this ministry. Plan fun activities for all age levels and promote fellowship among the congregation.

Forgiveness Ministry... All Christians are called to forgive; to assist in resolving conflict among the membership and to prevail where a need occurs. The forgiving spirit is a must for Christians, as Christ forgives us so it is with our forgiveness; **forgiveness is not an option, it is a must.**

Foster Care Ministry... Members in this ministry are loving and caring people. They have an innate desire to help children who need a family. They want to take on the responsibility and be a part of training up a child the way he/she should go.

Gardening Ministry... This ministry will plant a garden and give the veggies to the poor, needy, homeless shelters, sick and shut-in, etc. Churches are encouraged to purchase land for this purpose.

Get-Out-Of-The-Rut Ministry... Getting in a rut is somewhat normal in that we are creatures of habit. In an effort to remedy '**get out of the rut' situations,**' one must spiritually and assertively connect with others to concentrate on rut exit. Members may embrace each other as prayer partners in conjunction with the Embracement Ministry. Rut exit requires a commitment to change in the mind, heart and lifestyle of an individual.

Giving Ministry... The gift of giving is a wonderful gift and this is a marvelous ministry. Members with this gift welcome the opportunity to give to the church, charities and worthwhile causes. They cheerfully give of their money, themselves and resources. They want to help mankind, the environment and/or the animal kingdom; their giving is from the heart.

Good News Ministry... Pods of neighborhood children, under the age of eleven, gather with a church leader on a regular basis to be taught the ramifications of the Good News. They present an annual program to showcase the knowledge gained for parents and the community to enjoy.

Habitat for Humanity Ministry... The mission is well-known and the houses are so needed in most communities. The church, depending on the size, is capable of building one or more houses per year. This is a ministry where the entire membership can participate, either physically or monetarily. The blessings that flow from this effort and its partnerships are awesome.

Healing Ministry... This is another gift that is given to certain members of the Body of Christ. This ministry along with those who have great faith can make a difference by restoring health to the sick, apart from natural means. Individually, other healing methods are available to those who believe and share great faith. See the chapter on Prescriptions for Healing.

Helping Hand Ministry... Consideration is given to requests for help of any kind and a decision will be rendered by this ministry, as to which requests should receive a donation or help from the congregation.

Higher Hope Ministry... Encouraging Christians and others to keep looking to the hills from whence cometh our help and to forget about the things of this world. By keeping our eyes on Jesus, it lifts our spirit, it gives us the strength to overcome challenges and it helps the church to move forward.

Hobbies/Vintage Ministry... This ministry serves a dual purpose in that an interest in sharing one's passion for hobbies is eminent; a reminder that vintage pieces could deliver some very historical lessons for the young folks as well as monetary gain. Members will encourage young adults to begin collecting, if they have not already done so.

Hospitality Ministry...A constant reminder to all that any act of kindness is godly; so greeting members and visitors is a must. Members of this ministry could easily be involved with the evangelism and benevolent ministries. This gift embodies a high-level of interpersonal skills and a posture of kindness. Kindness is contagious and it draws people to Christ. Good manners are always in vogue.

Hymnody Ministry... Members will find ways to keep the old hymns alive and share their history. Some churches have hymn choirs and they have a designated time to render service.

Inspirational Key Chain Ministry... God's WORD is so powerful until it adds a blessing to the sick & suit-in, broken hearted, downtrodden, and to everyone who needs encouragement and a spiritual uplift. Type Bible verses, laminate them, individually cut them out, punch a hole in each and put them on a key-ring. Give them away or sell them. They may serve as a quick-fix in the time of need.

Intercessory Prayer Ministry... Intercessory prayer is a must for our Christian mission. *"The effectual fervent prayer of a righteous man (person) availeth much."* **(James 5:16b)** The Church family needs to pray for each other as well as the world at large.

Jail and Prison Ministry... Christians involved with this ministry will pray, teach and witness to an incarcerated population; it is definitely a Divine calling. This is a targeted population that is willing to listen because of their situation. Hope and encouragement are needed to help bring salvation to them.

Joy of My Salvation Ministry... New converts are so excited about finding Jesus until they need a ministry of their own. This opportunity affords them the privilege to share God's goodness, extend their friendship base and learn of Him together.

Junior Diaconate Ministry... From the children's church, those with leadership abilities will surface. This ministry will groom them for junior deacons and for those who continue to spiritually grow; they will eventually become leaders in the church.

Knowledge Ministry... Members with this gift are able to discover, analyze and clarify information for the well-being of the church. They are your Sunday school teachers, your church leadership members and others who cannot get enough of the **WORD**. Opportunities should be provided for these members to share some of their knowledge, analyze and clarify biblical information.

Kingdom Building Ministry... The church is tasked with the responsibility of extending God's Kingdom. The Great Commission declares that we are to help bring salvation to the lost. That is done in various ways; for starters, some of these ministries will be a big help as we go forth delivering random acts of kindness, witnessing for the Lord, and explaining to them that God loves them too.

Leadership and Administrative Ministry... This ministry will propel those with this gift to serve as leaders in the church; and assist other ministries to effectively implement strategies that will be about kingdom building and they are to work harmoniously with the entire church. The leadership model of Jesus Christ is recommended for leaders in the church in accordance with God's purpose for the future. The goals should be presented to the entire membership in hopes of ensuring working together harmoniously for the glory of God.

Lord's Supper Ministry... Preparation for the Lord's Supper is the primary responsibility for this ministry. During Holy Week, communion could be a special ceremony that deviates from the traditional ones. Churches may decide to have a candlelight ceremony with partakers dressed in white and the soulful hymns of long ago to help lift Jesus higher.

Loving Care for Senior Citizens Ministry... Many times the mature population of the church is inadvertently overlooked. This ministry focuses on doing some very good things for the older members. Helping them to continue to be viable, active members by accommodating some of their needs; such as, transporting them to church activities and out of town trips, help them to choose a ministry they would like to be a part of and visit with those who live alone.

Mark of Distinction Ministry... This ministry encourages the membership to live the life that is scripturally taught. As the old adage goes, "We should live the life we preach about" and stop diluting Christian values. The Mark of Distinction should be noted for its label; it is a dishonor to God to have any other agenda other than winning souls for Christ. They identify unmet needs and meet those needs.

Marriage Enrichment Ministry... Teaching couples about the provisions of a healthy marriage is the focus of this ministry. Offer programs and activities that will be spiritually enriching for individual families as well as the church family. Provide baby-sitting service one night annually to give couples a night to gather and enjoy each other.

Media Ministry... Record and Share media materials with congregation, the public and home bound members. Make use of available resources and diligently promote Christianity in a positive way that is innovative and pleasing to the Lord. The advancement of technology is making ministry a little easier for engagement of the membership. So think of creative ways to move Christianity forward in a timely manner.

Men's Fellowship Ministry... All men of the church are eligible for membership in this ministry. Oh, how beautiful it is for men to fellowship together. An aggressive plan of action would be in order to help with the Evangelism ministry by bringing other men to Christ. Establish an evangelism uniform that looks sharp, as it will serve as a magnet for generating interest. Mentor younger men, especially, those without fathers in the home and explain the expectations of manhood.

Mercy Ministry... Members with this gift feel empathy and compassion for people. They are your ministers, doctors, nurses, caregivers, etc. They go beyond the call of duty to help and they perform their duties cheerfully. They reflect on the fact that God gives us new mercies for each new day.

Multicultural Ministry... Different races of people and ethnic groups coming together to understand the many cultures that are present in our world for God is the creator. His intent is for all of us to get along and love one another. Racism, meaning all of God's people, is a welcome mat rather than a barrier for mankind..

Music Ministry... The main focus of this ministry is well-established, in that, it plays a major role with the worship services of the church. Recruit gifted singers and practice them often.

Music is a universal language that lifts the spirit and energizes the soul; beautiful music is becoming to heavenly angels. Some declared that Solomon understood the power of music. People today understand the power of music too.

Mustard Seed Ministry... Jesus Christ is credited as the founder of the mustard seed ministry. He began with twelve disciples and now the number is so great it is beyond our knowledge. Members will spread the gospel by planting mustard seeds in little children, teenagers and adults through Sunday school, mentoring, and in any venue that will allow participation. Seeds will be one or more promises from God, they are to stay with promises until fulfillment is met.

Neighborhood Ministry... An effort is made here to get to know our neighbors for the purpose of sharing interests, Bible study, neighborhood watch and scheduling events for families.

Networking Ministry... This ministry consists of members who are familiar with trends, the job market and share a willingness to help job seekers locate gainful employment. Also, they help to empower job seekers with needed career information. Start training the youth how to network at an early age.

New Members/Orientation Ministry... As a posture of Christian kindness from church members, this is the beginning of discipleship with new converts. The doctrine, mission and expectations are shared with new members to get them started on the right foot. This may be a review for some, but repetition is a very good reminder.

New Beginning Ministry... Starting over after you've had a knock-down **job** experience requires tenacity. Challenges and struggles will come because they are a part of living; however one must pick up the pieces and move forward. The encouragement found with this ministry is supported by the Scripture, "I will never leave you nor forsake you." In essence, we never walk alone; our helper is always by our side, just call on Him, He will answer. Remember that there is power in the name of Jesus.

Nuts & Bolts Ministry... Teaching and training the nuts and bolts on common things around the house; empowering people to help themselves by learning how to fix things; and save money in the process. There is a strong possibility that this training could be popular among widows, single women and those who are unable to handle these tasks. By helping members to acquire results, saves them money, now they will have additional monies to give to ministry.

Parenting Ministry... Tips and strategies are placed in a booklet along with other information on how to be a very good parent. This ministry will design and facilitate workshops/ seminars on parenting skills. A partnership with the local school district is a must to enable success. Develop an energizing carrot to encourage reluctant parents to become involved.

Pastoral Ministry... The gift of Pastor is a separate gift. It is far different from Evangelism, Teaching, Apostle and other gifts. Many try to include the gift of Pastor with those listed but Scripture has it listed as an individual gift; so not all preachers have the gift of Pastor. Pastors with this gift speak and treat their flock in a manner that is becoming to angels.

Pot Faith Dinner Ministry... At the designated time before prayer meeting and Bible Study, a meal is served. It can be done monthly or quarterly but it is a good time to fellowship and invite unbelievers... it is called the Pot Faith Dinner and that suggests faith is the focal point. Other ministries should help out when needed; tailor agenda to fit your congregation.

Praise and Clinging Power Ministry... Members will lead praise teams and congregation in praise, prayer, songs and inspire the Household of Faith to Hold on to God's Unchanging Hand. Encourage congregation to participate in singing praises to the Lord.

Preparation Ministry... Be ye also ready; ready for what? Ready to take advantage of every opportunity that comes down the pipeline. This requires preparation, preparation and more preparation. It doesn't matter what field of knowledge, vocation, or career that is chosen, preparation is the key. Members of this ministry have been there and done that, yet, they are willing to share resources, encourage interested parties, and help them to succeed. Please be reminded that Heaven is a prepared place for a prepared people, so prepare to take flight one day in your career, in your political aspiration, or to go home and live with Jesus.

Prosperity Ministry... Put your money in trust in the heavenly bank by helping people in need. Poverty is running rampant. God blesses a cheerful giver; one that sees a void and tries to fill the need. Members know that the Lord will supply their need according to His riches in glory.

Random Acts of Kindness Ministry... Diligently seek innovative ways to be kind to others. Surprise them with your goodness and humbly submit yourself under the mighty hand of God. He will send the needy your way and provide you with the necessary tools to implement your task.

Reconciliatory Ministry... The leadership will reach out to disenchanted members by way of this ministry. This ministry assumes the duty of touching base with those who have not been able to look beyond our faults and see Jesus on the cross. Develop a strategic plan to follow that will ensure fair treatment. Through meetings, conversations, obtaining an understanding and prayers of faith, a reconciliatory spirit will surface.

Recovery Ministry... Provide training for overcoming stumbling blocks that were ushered in by the forces of an unclean spirit, as regaining composure is in order. Redirect energy to a higher level of thinking will help to maintain a forward movement. Encouragement from those who share similar experiences validates recovery. Activate faith along the way and let the Lord have center stage; He is waiting and ready to assist.

Recreation, Fitness & Wellness Ministry... Keeping the mind, body and soul healthy are inclined to enhance longevity. A regular diet of God's WORD is very good for the soul but exercise is good for the body. Mature adults need to be encouraged to participate. Also this ministry is responsible for the children's recreation department.

Repentance Ministry... There is always a need to repent, since we are not perfect people. This ministry should encourage members, backslider and others to repent as often as necessary because it is the right thing to do. The Lord appreciates our honesty. Jesus began His ministry by saying, *"Repent: for the kingdom of heaven is at hand." (Matthew 4:17)*

Revival Ministry... Revivals are designed to give Christians a spiritual boost. Also, it is a method used in search of the lost; an invitation is given to come hear the Good News. A plan of action and other preparatory stimulants, prior to the revival, will ensure a progressive outcome. Partnering with the Evangelism and Prayer ministries will prepare membership for soulful revivals. Often times the Lord will send in a drunk, a thief, a drug dealer, and/or a big-time sinner to see how the church will treat this person. This is a test from God, please don't fail this test.

Saturday Night Live Ministry... This ministry is strictly for young folks. They hold Church every Saturday night, and rightly so, they serve as ushers, the choir, band, take up offerings and assist with virtually all parts of the service except for preaching. Normally, the Youth Pastor is charged with the duty of preaching or an invitation is given to other speakers. Encourage members to invite all the youth in the neighborhood to these services.

2 Chronicles 7:14 Ministry... This ministry is self-explanatory. *"If my people, which are called by my name, shall humble themselves, and pray, and seek my face, and turn from their wicked ways; then will I hear from heaven, and will forgive their sin, and will heal their land."*

Showcasing Talent Ministry... Encouragement is given to young folks to come forth and showcase their talents. Members will help nurture them and regularly put on talent shows. Monies raised from talent shows are donated to a worthy cause for the youth.

Single Parent Ministry...These parents realize that their task as a parent is awesome and they need a village to help raise a child. By sharing support, knowledge and wisdom with each other will bring some comfort to their encounters. Help these parents by sharing your resources.

Singles' Ministry...This ministry will create an atmosphere and design programs that are welcoming for singles. Examples: Singles Bible Study, singles bowling teams, singles Pot Faith Dinners, singles bus tours and many others. Keep in mind that they are in search of a mate.

Social Justice Ministry...The Church will become abreast of social justice issues as members in this ministry collaborate with leadership. The need to evoke corporate prayer on issues may involve the entire church. Encourage young members to become participants in civic leadership; it could serve as a viable learning tool.

Spiritual Fitness...Individually, one has to reckon with self to discern his spiritual fitness and answer the question have I surrendered all to Christ. Many times ego, pride and attitude become stumbling blocks that keep Jesus at a distance. To draw closer to Him requires getting rid of these vices by focusing on prayer and standing on His promises.

Spiritual Food Ministry...The soul needs to be fed; members will purchase and distribute BIBLES to jails, prisons, homeless shelters and other places where Bibles are needed. In general, the WORD should be shared in conventional and unconventional places.

Stewardship Ministry... Acting in partnership with Christ to manage all that we have and all that we are for the purposes and the glory of God. This ministry reminds the congregation that stewardship relates to your time, your talent and your tithe.

Sugar and Spice Ministry... This ministry is for the little children, it is commonly known as the Nursery Ministry. It specializes in letting the children know that the Church loves them by being kind, giving praise, and teaching them about the Gospel.

Sunday School Ministry... To motivate, encourage and teach people of all ages in Sunday school. Train teachers for this ministry and share some programs or activities for engagement in fellowship as a bonding exercise with other ministries. A blend of other related ministries will give this ministry a strong presence; it should consider holding Sunday school at other places where the un-churched gather.

Sweet Hour of Prayer Ministry... Prayer partners and prayer chain normally fall under this ministry. The prayer chain connects people to the needs of the membership and community. The chain is setup on paper first to establish method of execution. Prayer partners work better on an individual basis; yet, prayer chains work well when properly organized.

Teaching Ministry... Aside from the Sunday school lesson, the focus here is on topics for study that were submitted by members of the congregation. Teach in such a way that is understandable, and with this practical approach it helps members with their challenges by applying biblical concepts to their everyday situations.

Tithing Ministry…An integral part of Giving and Stewardship ministries is tithing; they should all work together for the good of the order. This ministry is inclusive of ten percent of our time, talent (gift) and money that should be given to the Church. Again, when the three are present, this is stewardship at its best. The mission of tithing is to help support church ministries.

Transportation Ministry…An outreach ministry that specializes in transporting children whose parents do not attend church. Also transport adults, members and others who need a ride to church functions, out of town activities and to facilitate transportation for all church activities.

Trustees Ministry…This leadership ministry is responsible for keeping the Church on a solid foundation; making good decisions financially by making assessments and evaluating progress. Moreover, trustees need to make sure the monies are placed in the proper places and bills are paid. Trustees may collaborate with deacons in making viable decisions. Trustees that are appointed by the Church should assume their duties as being very serious and not allow others to take over. Trustees should remember that all money given and collected for and by the Church is holy.

Tutorial Ministry…There is a need for some children to improve their test taking skills. This ministry may assist with teaching, remediation and testing.

Vacation Bible School Ministry…This ministry has been around for years; it is still viable and serving our youth in a mighty way. Each church will add a nugget to enrich its membership.

Visitation Ministry…Visits, as a unit or individually, will encourage and give spiritual uplift to believers and unbelievers;

the sick and elderly, as well as those who have encountered unfortunate situations. Assess needs and share this information with the appropriate ministry. With each visit, take something to cheer people, bless them and lift their spirits.

Volunteers / Servants Ministry...A dynamic ministry that will perpetuate servant-hood; we are called to be servants... meaning, simply find a need and fill the void. Service is the rent we pay for saying good morning. To whom much is given, much is required. Service and giving are so tightly woven until it is really hard to separate them. Know that you are always on the winning team as long as you are giving. None of it goes unnoticed by God.

Ways and Means Ministry... Members will work out the logistics and mechanics of any given situation for the Church by making sure the right decisions are made. Ways and Means members work closely with the trustees and deacons. They will facilitate and assist other church ministries with activities. They should be informed of everything that goes on in the church.

Widows' for Christ Ministry... Members will meet to witness, listen, pray, share and encourage one another. Plan activities that are church related and share wisdom with the young adults. The congregation must recognize and hold widows in high esteem as Christ has shown favor to Christian widows.

Wisdom Ministry... This special ability that is given to certain members of the church allows them to receive insight as a result of knowing the mind of the Holy Spirit. They tend to understand the Will of God and reflect on its impact to the church. Members in this ministry should be included on the nominating committee and the Discipleship ministry.

Women's Fellowship Ministry... All women of the church are eligible to participate in this ministry. They will provide services to accommodate their needs and pleasure, to enhance kingdom building as they work with other ministries and embrace the strategic plan of the church. They need to be visible in the community as they spread the Gospel.

Young Adult Ministry... Young adults between the ages of eighteen through thirty-nine belong in a caring unit with a focus on their needs. They will plan Christian related programs and activities that are age-specific. They must work with other outreach ministries by inviting other young adults to Church.

Comments: As the Lord leads, guides and abides with you, consider and participate in some type of ministry. Christians are called to do some work for the Lord. **A Divine call is your deepest spiritual pain.** It is a source of a special gift, spiritual strength and energy. For God's tacit voice demands the silence and response of your soul. So be willing to make a change, if you find yourself on the wrong road to nowhere, find another road to somewhere. This call will sustain you for battle as you go forth in dealing with lesser minds and evil spirits.

Christianity is a religion that gives us a Savior and a Comforter, the Holy Spirit lives within us. As you know, our Father's strategy is one of encounter; for it is hoped that difficult times will draw you closer to Jesus. Some Christians are already participating with in-house ministries, and that is very good. It is our prayer that the entire church will get busy and participate in one or more ministries. The Lord will be very pleased to see Christians busy with in-house and outreach ministries. **Christians will see the positive difference it will make in their lives. Be reminded that one day, each individual will become the 'least of these.' And whatever you sow, that you will definitely reap.** *"Be not deceived; God is not mocked: for whatsoever a man soweth, that shall he also reap." **(Galatians 6:7)***

If any man serve me, let him follow me; and where I am, there shall also my servant be: "if any man serve me, him will my Father honour." **(John 12:26)**

Acknowledgements

The graciousness of some people who are willing to be helpful is mind-boggling. A special thanks is due to Elaine Parke for the revelation on the future church as explained in this booklet.

Also, I extend gratitude to Glenda Simmons Jenkins for applying her editorial and proofreading skills to the final draft of this book manuscript.

A heartfelt thank you is given to both ladies.

About the Author

Helen Baker Britt has built a distinguished career in education. From media specialist and assistant principal to academic advisor, she has spent more than five decades working at all academic levels, most recently in post-secondary career counseling. Born in rural Nassau County, Fla., her roots in the close-knit Christian community there run deep. The daughter of a devout deacon and a praying missionary, Britt has followed their example in spreading good will. She has adopted prisons, hospitals and schools as her mission field. Distributing Bibles and leading workshops, Britt has applied her professional skills and her passion for discipleship, ministry and outreach to the personal and spiritual growth of inmates, invalids and students. Her creativity and imagination in developing unique ministries is one of Britt's strongest gifts. Since retiring in 2012, she has continued to fuel her God-given passion for ministry by launching a key chain outreach that offers encouragement to people in their relationship with Christ. Britt holds a bachelor's degree in Library

Science from Florida A&M University, Tallahassee, and a master's degree in Curriculum and Instruction with certification in Administration and Supervision from the University of South Florida in Tampa.

We forgot to mention that her late husband was a deacon and a local politician.

Note to Readers:

A very popular question: If you have been with Jesus, where is your evidence?

Printed in the United States
By Bookmasters